"For good or ill, we leave our mark on society and our world. Therefore, if we really do want to leave this world a better place for others to live in (for what else is the purpose of living?), then we are ready to believe that the family is the place to begin . . .

"The pleasure of belonging to a family is a treasure indeed. Each person needs a place where he or she belongs. This, then, is the joy of belonging to a family: We can relax in a private place, whether it is a tent or a tower, a condominium, a cottage, or a castle, with people who love us as we are. When we take a positive attitude toward the home and family, we see the pleasure that is there for us to enjoy.

"The basic problem with the American family today is that we've stopped looking! We've stopped talking! We've stopped touching! If we are to heal the hurts of our nation, let's begin with the family . . ."

—from *The Positive Family*

1]0667786

ARVELLA SCHULLER

THE POSITIVE FAMILY

A JOVE BOOK

TO

Robert Harold Schuller,

without whom this book would not be possible

Excerpt from the hymn "Hold Thou My Hand" composed by
C. S. Briggs used by permission of The Boston Music Co.,
Boston, MA.

This Jove book contains the complete
text of the original hardcover edition.

THE POSITIVE FAMILY

A Jove Book / published by arrangement with
Doubleday and Company, Inc.

PRINTING HISTORY
Doubleday-Galilee edition published 1982
Jove edition / August 1983
Third printing / March 1984

ISBN: 0-515-08091-8

Jove books are published by The Berkley Publishing Group,
200 Madison Avenue, New York, N.Y. 10016.
The words "A JOVE BOOK" and the "J" with sunburst
are trademarks belonging to Jove Publications, Inc.
PRINTED IN THE UNITED STATES OF AMERICA

CONTENTS

I

A FAMILY! WHAT'S THAT?

My husband and I were sitting in a quaint little lakeside restaurant in Lucerne, Switzerland. The setting sun was casting a colorful path across the glassy lake. Two swans glided smoothly across the blue surface, which mirrored the purple mountains encircling it.

Inside, the warm glow of lamps gave a homey atmosphere which was highlighted by friendly conversations overheard from neighboring tables. A few feet from us a large table was expectant of a special party. Places were set for at least twelve persons. Fresh flowers adorned the very center.

Soon they came—an old, a middle-aged, and a young couple. It was obvious that this was a family party. Was it a birthday for the mother and grandmother?

We understood very little of the German language, but we *did* understand the love and joy that flowed from that corner of the room for the remainder of the evening. We found ourselves rejoicing with them when laughter interrupted our conversation. And though they were complete strangers, we felt a warm bond with their affection, admiration, and oneness with each other.

How different from another family incident that we shall not soon forget.

"Surely, someone will come to the funeral," my husband replied optimistically. "Let's wait a little longer before we begin the liturgy." A half hour passed. Forty-five minutes passed. Not one relative, neighbor, or friend came.

The mortician had telephoned our home a few days earlier with the familiar request, "Would your husband be available to conduct a simple burial service for an older gentleman?"

My husband agreed and at the set hour arrived at the funeral home. The undertaker briefed him on the details of the service, and then with great concern said, "I doubt if there will be any relatives, friends or neighbors in attendance." He went on to explain that not one person had come to pay respects. Yes, there were three sons living in the area, but the funeral arrangements had been handled completely by telephone.

Not one son came to bury his father. Not one friend came to say goodbye. Not one neighbor came to say a prayer!

It was the *saddest* and most *unusual* funeral my husband ever officiated at; he and the undertaker were the only two persons who attended the service.

What a contrast in these two family events. Why? What makes the difference between family members who really enjoy one another and family members who want to deny the very existence of the rest of their family, and the family as an organization or institution?

I trust that in the pages of this book I will be able to communicate the need and the importance of looking at the family through "positive eyes."

We hear much today about the effects on our health of positive versus negative thinking. In school and sports, we see exciting results of a positive mental attitude. But I want to share what I have learned about the happy life-style that comes from applying a positive mental attitude within the family circle.

THE FAMILY—THE MOST IMPORTANT
UNIT IN SOCIETY

There are negative voices in society today that describe the family as "a field of misunderstanding where people at different stages of human development speak to each other with mutual incomprehension."[*]

Then there are the confused voices in our world today who are asking questions such as:

The family—who needs it?
Can the family as a unit survive the twentieth century?

And, yes, there are the positive believers, to whom I belong. Let go of the family? No—let's go with the family! The *price* of the family? No—the *prize* of the family! We are certain that the family as a unit will not only survive but thrive. It is that most important force that puts meaning into life and work. It was therefore no surprise to read in a Harris survey (January 2, 1981) that 96 *percent* of polled Americans listed "having a good family life" as their *first* New Year's resolution. Only 18 percent listed "making a lot of money" as their first priority.

Svetlana, the daughter of the Russian leader Joseph Stalin, was interviewed on a talk show shortly after she arrived in America. She was asked the question, "What is one of the most difficult adjustments you face in our American lifestyle?" She quickly answered, "To be faced with so many choices! In Russia everything is decided for you, but here each day there are so many choices!"

What a precious freedom we enjoy, but making the right choice also carries with it an awesome responsibility.

What is your definition of the family? Which of these words best describe yours?

[*] Jacques Lacan, French psychologist, *New York Times Book Review*, February 24, 1980.

A force or a farce?
Peacemaker or pressure cooker?
Monarchy or anarchy?
Small group or loners' hangout?
Compatible or combatable?
Existing or enjoying?
Faltering or fulfilling?
Knots or nots?
Picnic or panic?

Choosing to view our families with a positive attitude is the only way we will succeed at having a good family life, and the only way we will enjoy our homes and families. In the forthcoming pages you will see how some families succeed and why. You will see that when the family becomes a team it hits a home run. And it is my hope that, by reading and then by practicing, we may learn to enjoy the intimate world of the family.

THE TREASURE OF THE FAMILY

In 1969, a Christmas card we received from one of our friends included a personally written note to our family. Their greeting ended with this beautiful sentence: "We are so thankful for our family and our lives together. The chances we have to *risk together, solve together, learn together, work together, play together, laugh together, cry together and pray together* have brought *joy* and *love* in *unending dimensions to our lives.*"

What a precious treasure the Almighty created when He planned the human family—sharing together, loving together, growing together, building together.

What is a family? To the positive believer, it is a colony of caring—two or more individuals caring very deeply for each other. A family, then, is a group of people who, when you hurt, show that they care. You *know* they care!

"To be lonely is to be lost!" said the young unmarried man

sitting across the breakfast table through handsome eyes brimming with tears as he looked at my husband and me. He did not elaborate on his revealing statement but quickly changed the subject, a little embarrassed by his emotions.

Belonging to a family assures that we need never be lonely or lost, for we are surrounded by those who love us and care deeply for us. I like to call this our "treasure of assurance."

"Home is the place where, when you have to go there, they have to take you in." Through the years, these words from the beloved poet Robert Frost have sparked in me an amused and understanding attitude—as I have watched the family come home, one by one—happy or sad, angry or "hyper," fighting or withdrawn. Anyone who lives in a family knows the many moods that cross the thresholds of our homes each day, but because we are a "colony of caring," we open the door, hold out our arms and we love!

What is a family? To the positive believers it is a colony of caring, a priceless treasure.

When we care about each other, we *show* that we care. In our first year of marriage my husband learned that I had a special love for a certain brand of chocolate turtles. One day when he came home from work, he made a special production of presenting me with two such chocolates in a bright paper bag. That was all he could afford. If I remember correctly, they cost fifteen cents each. This little gift-giving ceremony was such a precious moment that it became an instant tradition.

Now, once a year, my husband still presents me with a gift of my favorite brand of chocolate turtles. I eat them oh, so sparingly, not so much because of my diet, but because I want to savor the memory of his special gesture of caring, thirty years ago.

When we take a positive look at the family, we discover that the family is a treasure chest of people who are caring deeply for each other—so deeply that they go out of their way to do something beautiful for each other day after day, year after year.

"A compliment a day keeps insecurity away" is a favorite saying of mine and its importance was confirmed by Dorothy DeBolt, a very special person whom I admire greatly. I first met her four years ago when she visited our campus. She and her husband, Bob, have accomplished the ultimate in families. In her book *Nineteen Steps up the Mountain,* which she wrote shortly after their visit to us, she introduces you to her most inspiring family. The DeBolts have adopted thirteen severely handicapped children. Each is assigned specific household chores according to his or her own ability. Those who have no legs are responsible for sit-down tasks. The blind children are also given chores to do. During her visit Dorothy shared with us a ritual that is, in my opinion, the most important practice or habit a family can adopt. The DeBolts have a "building-up" time when they each answer the question, "What do I like about myself?" The positive, image-building statements offered by these handicapped children and young people were an inspiration to us; they seemed proof of the invaluable worth of positive thinking.

What is a family? A cluster in which each member is a builder of another, for the *I AM* must precede the *I CAN.*

As encouragement to young mothers, I write two simple lines. They are easy to memorize, and, if repeated often, they are able to help you through the worst of days:

> Some men build bridges, other tall skyscrapers—
> But a mother builds a leader for tomorrow's world.

The family of a child who grows up believing that he or she is a somebody, born with a uniqueness, has discovered a precious treasure! Believing that no two individuals are alike, that each is designed by God, gives a sense of awe and wonderment to children and parents alike.

It doesn't take long for parents of more than one child to realize that they can't treat them all the same. Each child responds differently to discipline. What works for one doesn't work for another. Each child is motivated by different goals, rewards, or punishments. Try cooking for a family of nine for a while. Your culinary efforts will receive every imaginable form of feedback. There is always one in the bunch who can't stand cucumbers, another who hides green olives under the rim of the plate, another who wants to eat nothing but ice cream. The family, as a cluster, was designed by the Creator to give the individuals within that unit the treasure of knowing and believing that each one is a special someone.

> I am somebody for
> I am God's child—
> I may be white
> I may be black
> I may be rich
> I may be poor
> But I am somebody, for
> I am God's child!

My husband often refers to our family as a special kingdom, known as the Schuller Kingdom. He is the king, I am his queen, our son is a prince, and each of our daughters is a princess.

The I AM precedes the I CAN. . . . When we believe in ourselves, we begin to discover the potential within us. *Then,* because the family supports us, believes in us and cares for us, we dare to try to achieve the "I CANS." If we fail, we rest assured that they will continue to love us.

THE PLEASURE OF THE FAMILY

Take a long positive look at the family, and we discover not only the *treasure,* but we enjoy the *pleasure* that comes from belonging to and caring for each other.

If we go out of our way to bring pleasure to each other, we begin to create a pleasant atmosphere within the four walls we call home. What pleases the other members of our family? Are we considerate in taking the time to find out their personal likes and dislikes?

As we get to know one another—our spouses and our children—we see what things bring a spontaneous smile and what things are left unnoticed. And we begin to realize that it is often not the big and flashy remembrances or kindnesses that prompt the pleasures of the heart, but the small, "little extras" that loudly shout "This is home. You belong here. We love you."

Traveling through northern Norway, the land of the midnight sun, Bob and I were shocked at the barrenness of the countryside. When the sun doesn't rise for three straight months and for another three months it never sets, no trees can survive. The mountains and hills are spotted here and there with scrawny bush. The village streets, lined with wooden structures, include no trees—anywhere. But as we walked along what seemed like desolate landscape, we spotted a red geranium blooming radiantly in the window of a home. I looked for others, and then I noted that in Hammerfest, the northernmost city in Europe, the front window of each home displayed one or more brightly blooming flowers.

It reminded me of my childhood farm home in northwest Iowa. Although we had no set of matching china, no silver, serving dishes and no linens for our table, fragrant lilacs picked from our bush or a small bowl of wild violets often added a fragrant beauty and special richness to the atmosphere of our home. The small efforts that brought life into our otherwise ordinary lives have never been forgotten.

"Home is the place where, when you have to go there, they have to take you in." What a comfort that statement brings when we arrive home from work. We close the door behind us to shut out that world of pressure and deadlines. We throw off our shoes; we enjoy the pleasure of home.

In 1970, when our littlest one was only three years old, I embarked upon a full-time career. Fortunately I was able to set my own work schedule around the school schedules of the children, including little Gretchen, who was enjoying preschool, three mornings a week. At the same time, a lovable California grandma came into our lives and hearts. She was lonely and lost following the sudden death of her husband, and our family helped give her a reason to go on living. She was a very special someone in our home for about four years, until her health failed. She was then no longer available to bake for us her delicious cinnamon rolls and warm custard, to tell us her unusual stories and share with us the beautiful prayers she had memorized from her Episcopal prayer book.

Mom Schug, as we called her, was that special person who made our home a pleasant place to come to, for all of us. She was a heavenly angel who gave our family indescribable pleasure.

The very existence and presence of my children make home a pleasure for me. When I've come home tired, only to open the door and hear their feet running toward me and feel their warm arms encircle my legs, I've thanked God for their life. They loved me without noticing when my dress was not the latest fashion, my hair needed attention, or I had a run in my stocking. They never noticed when my face was badly in need of some fresh makeup; they just loved me the way I was.

What a pleasure my family has been to me throughout these thirty mothering years. They have loved me when I've been tired or cross, pregnant or skinny. Sitting in a big chair and holding them in my arms, or, now that they are too big to snuggle on my lap, sitting beside them on the couch or around our dinner table with them, is truly one of the greatest pleasures of my life.

Our four daughters have never outgrown the pleasure of sitting on their daddy's lap, even though the oldest is in her late twenties, and neither has *he* outgrown the pleasure of knowing his girls want to sit on his lap!

The pleasure of belonging to a family is a treasure indeed. Each person needs a place where he or she belongs. That is a natural need for every human being. You and I gravitate to a place that we can call our own, a place where we can hang our hat, where we can live in privacy. Where I can be me! We naturally are pulled toward a person or group of persons whom we can trust, and where we are accepted as we really are. This, then, is the joy of belonging to a family: We can relax in a private place, whether it is a tent or a tower, a condominium, a cottage, or a castle, with people who love us as we are. When we take a positive attitude toward the home and family, we see the pleasure that is there for us to enjoy.

THE MEASURE OF THE FAMILY

A positive look at the family is not complete in only discovering the *treasure* and enjoying the *pleasure* of the family. We must also recognize the *measure* of influence our family has upon us as individuals, upon the world in which we live, and upon future generations.

When someone rises to a high position in world leadership and influence, the first information the world wants to know is, "What is the family history?" What culture or life-style has caused the talent or creative ability in this particular celebrity? Which persons influenced his or her character? What was and is the home life like?

Upon reading only a few of the volumes of biographies of well-known people, one will quickly sense that indeed the family—the home *and* the individuals in it—or the *lack* of family—greatly influences the actions and life changing decisions of adults and young persons. It makes them who they are, and in turn, the family molds and shapes future generations.

Name the person or persons who have shaped our world in art or music, politics or science. Look beyond those persons to the families and homes that molded them. We cannot fully measure the effect of the family, any family. Like the wake of a ship that leaves an unending ripple in an enormous sea, a family's influence can extend far beyond our sight or knowledge.

How are you and I being shaped as individuals within our families? What kind of persons would we have become had our family members been nonexistent—or if we had been brought up in some family other than the one we know?

How can you and I measure the influence upon us of the families that lived before our time? Our ancestors? Or even those who are not in our direct line, but whose lives affected those who were?

When I notice my husband's gestures, I see how much they resemble his uncle's, yet this amazes me, because they have lived worlds apart from each other until recently. My husband has been told that he is an unbelievably close image of his maternal great grandfather—in looks, character, drive, and positive attitude.

We compare our four daughters: two are blond, and have hazel eyes. Their build and drive are similar to each other. The other two daughters have dark hair and brown eyes. Their skin texture is the same. They even pout and think alike. Their genes have influenced them more than they may know.

There comes a time in the life of each of us when we look in the mirror and ask the questions:

Who am I?
Where have I come from?
Where am I going?

More than one of our family's friends have been adopted children. Their origins are unknown to them. We have watched as they have struggled and suffered with the mysterious haunting unanswered questions:

Who are my parents?
Why did they not keep me?

Even though these friends of ours were adopted by homes in which they were surrounded with love and understanding, it is difficult for them to believe they are really "O.K.," to obtain the necessary degree of self-worth and self-love that every person needs in order to function normally in the arena of life.

What is a family? The family is a force of influence. We
need to ask, can we measure the influence of the family as an
organized force on planet earth? We live in a universe with
an organizational structure. Our planet, earth, is made up of
continents, then countries. They are broken down into states
or provinces, then counties, cities or towns, families or homes,
and then individuals.

In many cultures it is still unusual for a single individual to
live alone. On the death of a family member, the larger family unit becomes the intimate family. We were reminded of
this in New Guinea, where, in 1972, we studied the family life
of this primitive population. In fact, these tribes were so
primitive that they believed that if, when someone in the family died, they ate the inside organs of the deceased, they
would thereby grant their loved one "eternal life." This
resulted in a devastating physical illness called "the laughing
disease," which most often was fatal. Yet with all of their indescribable customs and rituals, there was a fierce loyalty to
the family and the next of kin. In this culture, when the husband and father of a family was killed, the brother took the
widow and children as his own. This, of course, is an ancient
custom and beautifully described in the Old Testament story
of Ruth and Boaz.

We often hear the cliché "Blood is thicker than water," and
we need only study history books to see the measure of the
family on world events: inventions, movements, pioneering
new worlds and continents, and, yes, wars.

May I suggest then that we take a serious look at the positive influence of our family upon ourselves, our community
and especially the next generation. As an individual or collec-
tively the family is the world shaper of the future.

Bruno Bettelheim, the world-renowned psychoanalyst, has
spent over forty years at the University of Chicago in the
study of "generativity," the responsibility for the next generation, guiding the young in their preparation as leaders of their
society.

He is much concerned with our modern western society. He

sees us as a society whose members lack a strong sense of morality, and thus as an endangered species. Bettelheim believes that many problems of today's young and old are rooted in the fact that no moral system has a powerful hold on the public imagination. We are all engaged in a desperate search for meaning. He believes that this "meaning" can only come from within the self. And then it can be projected outward into the world.*

An illustration that I heard many years ago clearly sums up this point:

A father came home from a hard day at work. He wanted to do nothing but relax. His little boy came running to him saying, "Daddy, Daddy, come and play with me!"

But Daddy was too tired, so, trying to distract the boy for a few minutes, he replied, "Johnny, I want you to do something for me. Run and bring me the world globe off my desk, and also the map that is right beside it!"

"Okay, Daddy," and Johnny triumphantly returned with both the globe and map. In a moment Daddy had ripped the map to shreds, with a puzzled Johnny watching at his side.

"Now, Johnny, I want you to match up and paste the torn map to the globe," the father said.

Giving himself a pat on the back for thinking up a project that would keep the boy occupied for a whole evening, he contentedly settled back for a long nap.

Much to his dismay, Johnny was back at his side in five minutes. The map was accurately pieced together, and in place on the globe. The astonished father sat up in amazement!

"How did you finish such a difficult job so quickly?"

"It was easy, Daddy," was Johnny's reply. "See, there is a little boy on the back side of the map, and *when you get the boy put all together, the world falls into place too.*"

For good or ill, we leave our mark on society and our world. Therefore, if we really do want to leave this world a

* *Psychology Today,* July 1981.

better place for others to live in (for what else is the purpose of living?), then we are ready to believe that the family as society's smallest group is the place to begin to improve our world. Look through these next pages that show how a positive family works. You'll discover the treasure of the family, the pleasure of the family, and the measure of the family.

2

WHERE SHOULD
WE START?

"I had it all backward! We were lovers first; then we tried to become friends, and it didn't work."

A cynical mood dominated the conversation as the young husband related how his two-year-marriage was finished and there seemed little hope of a reconciliation.

My heart sank as I listened in surprised dismay to what began as a casual greeting with this friend of ours as we stood in line at a neighboring supermarket.

"I had it all backward . . . ," he repeated. "Next time, if there ever is a next time, I'll make sure we are friends first, then as a relationship grows beyond friendship, I'll consider marriage." Pausing, hanging his head in remorse, he said, "Then, and only then, will I take her to bed."

Where should we start? For if we don't start right, we won't end up right.

One morning as I rushed to the office for my first appointment of the day, I buttoned the jacket of my suit while driving down the freeway. As I opened the door to our building, the receptionist smiled and greeted me with a "Good morning, Mrs. Schuller," but I noticed an amused look on her face.

I hurried down the corridor to my office, where my secretary laughingly greeted me with "It looks like you started off wrong this morning; if you don't begin right, you won't end up right." She pointed to my jacket, which had one button protruding from the bottom and the extra buttonhole gaping at the neck.

How true those words are! To attain success in family life, it is necessary that we begin in right order. There is a right order in the universe and in life, and we find success easier when we start it out right.

Where should we start? If we are to begin to succeed in family relationships, we need to understand that there is a positive and a negative way of thinking, talking, and living.

I often hear the remark, "If it doesn't work out, we'll get a divorce." When the first crisis or problem develops, we are already programmed by society to say, "We must be incompatible. A divorce is our only solution." A negative attitude programmed into our subconscious becomes a negative act.

"Why do we treat the ones we love the most the worst?"

Here in the private corridors of the home, where we see each other as we really are, we often feel that all the rules society has imposed on us do not apply. Here we act as if we had the right to discard normal social restraints. Are we overreacting to the rigid rules of our community? Our place of work or worship? Are we developing a "devil-may-care" attitude trying to find our "real" self when no one who really matters is looking? Do we believe that we need to be crude and rude in order to be honest about our own feelings? Is it possible that we have never learned to distinguish between positive and negative living?

Someone asked me recently, "When we live in a world that is ninety-five percent negative—out there on the street, in the store, the office, the classroom, and even in the church—then how can our family really be positive?"

My answer was simple. "It is our choice to think, talk, and act in a positive or in a negative mood, method, and manner. The very basis of a successful marriage and family begins here: cultivate a growing sensitivity and consciousness of positivism versus negativity.

Once we grasp the *importance* of the positive attitude in home and family relationships, then we need to *understand* what being positive really means.

Being positive doesn't mean that we become *namby-pamby* parents, or that our homes become a chaos of undisciplined living, but it is recognizing that each crisis and every problem —small or large—presents us with a choice. How true it is then that each crisis and every problem is a challenge to grow! We can choose a positive or a negative reaction!

About a year ago, after I had finished conducting a motivational seminar for young mothers, a lovely member of the class came to me and tearfully shared how "just yesterday, my kindergartner came home with a progress report that was disgraceful. I angrily sent him to his room and would not allow him to play with his friends for the remainder of the day. I did not ask him why he had done so poorly or give him a chance to tell his side of the story. I believed the worst about him and I sent him to bed last night without giving him a single compliment or letting him know I loved him. I now see how negatively I was reacting. I'm going home and changing my attitude!"

Even today, after reading report cards for twenty-five years, I still notice the C's and D's before I notice the A's and B's. I notice the "*Needs to improve*" before the E's for excellence. However, I've progressed enough to compliment and congratulate the children on their high marks before I *ask* why the low mark. What causes that D or F to leap out at us in such large letters? I have learned that it is my own negative attitude, my fear of failing as a parent, that makes me overreact.

How positive are you?
. . . when the alarm rings in the morning?
. . . when your partner is late?
. . . when dinner burns beyond recognition?

. . . when you have a flat tire on the freeway?

. . . when there is too much month left over after your money is gone?

. . . when the baby cries all night?

. . . when your teenager comes in after curfew?

More than once in our thirty-one years of marriage, I have heard my husband say, as our family sat down to dinner, "Honey, you ask the blessing tonight." Usually there was an amused look on his face as he saw I was serving his "un-favorite" casserole. He learned this "positive" reaction to a seemingly negative situation from the late Peter Marshall. It has turned our dinner hour into a happy time instead of a pouting, complaining hour.

Yes! A *positive* thought always leads to a *positive act*, while a *negative* thought always results in a *negative act*.

It was a hot afternoon and the corridor was crowded. During the intermission of a Saturday-afternoon concert, my youngest daughters, Gretchen and Carol, and I waited impatiently in a long line at the drinking fountain.

Suddenly tension filled the air, as we saw and heard the loud slap of a mother's hand across the head of a five-year-old girl, "Dummy, why didn't you stay behind me? Now we've lost our place in line!"

I shuddered and a quiet sadness crept over the three of us. The real loss was not the place in line. The positive self-image of this child took a more severe beating than the child's head. I wondered if this lovely child would become what her mother thoughtlessly, in anger, named her. For I remembered what a young teenaged girl had recently told me.

She slouched across the table from me in the coffee shop near the office. I guessed her to be about fifteen—overweight, with long brown unkempt hair falling down to the shoulder buckles of her baggy overalls.

"May I ask you a question, Mrs. Schuller? Dr. Schuller and you always talk about positive thinking, but how does it work for someone like me, who is a dummy? I get bad grades in school. No guys ever ask me out because I'm so ugly. If I think positive, I'm still not going to get better grades. I was born a dummy and that's what I always will be!"

After a few get-acquainted sentences, I launched into what our teens would call a "telling off." But Susan hung on to every word as if she were starved and I was handing her food. I tried to pull the deep hurt from within her.

"First of all, what's your name? Susan? Okay—Susan, I don't believe that God makes dummies. We all have different mental ability and intelligence, but you excel in an area where I am a 'dummy' and I excel in an area where you would have difficulty. Neither you nor I begin to use even ten percent of the brain cells we have been given. You may be having a hard time fitting into the school's program. But that does not make you a dummy!

"As for being ugly, your features are as pretty as any, and your hair is a beautiful, beautiful color. Your eyes and face are lovely. But your negative self-image is the unattractive part of you. It causes you to be overweight and your facial expressions and body language shout out, 'I don't like myself.'

"You need positive thinking soaked into every brain cell you have. So here is my prescription: You may *never* call yourself a dummy again. If you do, you are insulting God. Each morning look yourself in the mirror and say aloud, 'Susan, you have perfect features. Your hair is a beautiful color. Your complexion is flawless. Your eyes and smile are super. You are a lovely girl—if you *think* you are.' That, Susan, is the first step. You need to convince *yourself* and then the insecurity will fade. The confidence you will begin to feel is the secret to your beauty."

I couldn't help but feel that if Susan had grown up in a positive family environment, she would have become a knock-out, for when the positive mental attitude becomes a positive act, a positive life-style invades a family's environment. The persons in that comfortable environment become creative, beautiful people full of respect for each other. They have open minds to new ideas, especially in times of stress and tension.

Yes, the positive approach has worked miracles in our family for over thirty years. I'd like to share more fully our family's "secrets" to a successful home life. My husband, Bob, and I are just average people with faults not much different from yours, yet our attitudes have changed our most difficult days into meaningful joy-filled memories.

3

UNCHANGING ROLES IN A CHANGING WORLD

When we were first married, Bob and I each had our own particular roles clearly defined for us by our background and culture.

Without any discussion, we both assumed that I, as the wife, would cook, keep the house clean, do the laundry, and care for the children. Meanwhile, Bob would earn the bread and butter, pay the bills, carry out the trash, do any repair job, clean the garage, and be responsible for the car.

Our individual roles were neatly kept in two boxes, one marked "his" and the other "hers." Now, thirty years later, the two boxes have become one circle of responsibility tied with a ribbon of love. After years of adjustment and change, we enjoy a relaxed peace about each other's many roles.

It's so interesting to watch our children's roles change as they begin their families. Our son is already an expert at changing diapers, a chore that my husband never did master (perhaps if Pampers had been on the market, he would have done better). Our son thinks nothing of getting breakfast for the family and dressing their daughter and taking her to school while his wife goes to her place of business or to class pursuing her education.

Today I've become almost as efficient as my husband when it comes to repairing an electric cord or attaching the drapery rods. And he can do a pretty good job of cleaning up the kitchen or tossing a salad.

We do not see these physical tasks or skills as being "male" or "female." We all pitch in to get the work done. These traditional roles may or may not work for you, but we should never be hesitant to learn each other's jobs, for then we can best show our love for each other.

If we are not afraid of change, the shifting roles can bring positive results. Perhaps I do not fear change because I have seen so much of it in my lifetime. In just a few short years, technology has turned our world upside down.

As a farm girl, I cooked on a woodburning stove, used an outhouse as the only toilet, hauled all of the water for drinking or washing from a well quite a distance away, and studied by lamplight (not having electricity in our home until I was a teenager). The children believe that I actually lived in the "Little House on the Prairie" days. I even pinch myself once in a while as I push a button and walk out of the kitchen, only to return to sparkling-clean dishes, then push two more buttons in the laundry room and my clothes are automatically cleaned and dried. I push another button and my microwave oven cooks an apple or boils water in one minute. Recently I heard about a domestic robot—a programmed computer that awakens you in the morning, tells you the time, the weather, the latest news and puts on the coffeepot.

"You've come a long way, baby" is the song I should continually sing.

— from lamplight to TV
— from the country phone to computer
— from the Model T Ford to the Concorde.

I still remember our first automobile, a Model T Ford. What excitement reigned on our farm that day. All of our family proudly took turns putt-putting on the country road. And I remember the trip from Paris, France, to Washington,

D.C., on the Concorde when in '76 we traveled at Mach 2–1400 miles an hour. When we lifted from the ground, the night was black and as the streamlined plane sped westward, we watched the sky grow lighter and brighter until we caught up with the sunset.

We need not—and must not—fear changing roles within a changing world, *if* our priorities are in the right order.

PRIORITIES: THE FAMILY COMES FIRST

About eight years ago, while my husband was finishing a writing assignment, he asked that I attend an executive management course in his place. I could take notes for him, he said, but as an addendum to his request he suggested that I might gain some know-how for my own areas of business. Timidly and curiously, I went to the first lecture of the six-week course. I was one of two women in the class. The professor began by stating that the first week of studies would be focused on "the *priorities* of the executive". During the next four days I listened carefully and quietly. What would he see as the priorities that promised success? I kept hearing the bottom line as "your family comes first and your business is in second place."

Your family first, your business second. Was I hearing the professor accurately? After class was dismissed on the fifth morning, I inched my way forward, and asked him, "Am I hearing you correctly? Are you telling the class that if they want to be successful in business their family must come first? I don't understand."

"You heard correctly!" His answer was direct and immediate. "It is a proven fact," he continued, "that executives who value their families more than their businesses have their priorities in correct order. Those executives are far more productive. Their creative energy is greater and they are far more relaxed and confident."

I couldn't wait to get home to give this news to my husband. I sensed that I was *very important* to my husband, but I hadn't known that I was supposed to be first place—*above* his career.

I must give credit to a special person who, five years after our marriage, helped me rearrange my priorities into the right order. That person is Mrs. Norman Vincent Peale.

I had long admired and respected this leader, and now I would have an opportunity to meet her personally. How should I act? I felt awestruck in her presence. After some nervous moments for me, I asked her the question that had been burning on my lips. I was so curious to know more about her interests. "Mrs. Peale, what are your latest and newest projects?"

I shall never forget her long pause and the way she looked me directly in the eye. I knew she strongly believed in whatever she was about to say. "I have only *one* project," she said confidently, "and *He* is my *Husband!*"

I gulped! I remember nothing of the remainder of our conversation, but I went home and took a serious look at my priorities. I was involved in all kinds of worthy and noble projects, but when the list of all of my commitments was completed, I had to admit that my husband and family received my leftover time, of which there was very little.

Hearing Mrs. Peale's firm statement of purpose became a turning point for me. From that time to this—for twenty-five years—I rearranged my priorities as follows: Husband first; children second; career third; music fourth; volunteer organizations fifth. What a difference this one major choice has made in my ability to relax in my daily scheduling decisions. And I have reason to believe it has contributed substantially to the harmonious, fruitful, and tension-free marriage we've had ever since.

One day I was asked to speak to a group of some fifty to sixty husbands on a specific topic, "What I need from my husband!"

I began by sharing the priorities in relationships and careers that are central to Bob and my marriage. I elaborated how necessary it was for me to be first place in my husband's priorities and he in mine. When I explained that we set apart one night each week just for the two of us, I was interrupted by the raised hand of a distinguished-looking gentleman. He took issue with the importance of this practice. "But I do not have *time* to spend dating my wife each week," he maintained. "After all, we have a teenage daughter. It is my duty to be a good father to her, and so we spend an evening together at a sports event or a movie. There just aren't enough evenings for me to also spend one alone with my wife."

With as much conviction in my face and voice as Mrs. Peale had shown in hers, I asked him a question, "In only a few years your daughter will be old enough to leave home. She will probably find herself a man who will, believe it or not, mean more to her than you do. When she says, ''Bye, Daddy,' where will you be? Will you be able to talk with your wife? Or will the two of you be strangers who are in different worlds?"

No wonder many marriages break up in the twenty-year period simply because children are gone. Get your priorities in the right order!

Along with a positive look at changing roles, we must emphasize that there are certain roles that remain unchanged through the years. No matter how computerized our society becomes, there will always be a need for you and me to continue to fulfill those roles to make our world a happier place to live.

May I suggest that the first unchanging role is that of *comforter*.

THE COMFORTER

A changing world is a hurting world. Whenever there is change, there comes tremendous insecurity and fear. "How can I cope?" is a question I hear again and again.

Husbands fear that wives will change, and vice versa; parents fear that teens will become strangers. Life-styles change through professions, careers, or moving to a new community or state, or through growth that occurs simply through a new hobby or project. Even joining a new club or volunteer organization can rock your family's boat and can cause fear or insecurity in other family members. So see yourself in the positive role of the comforter to your husband or wife, comforter to your children, comforter to your larger family, comforter to your employees, comforter to your neighbors, comforter to the world at large.

The first rule I have in my role as comforter is: *Never be negative.*

One morning during my "think" time, I came across the words written by the wisest of the wise. From the book of Proverbs I read: "A dry crust eaten in peace is better than steak every day along with argument and strife."

Of all the many beautiful things I could do for my family—any gift I might purchase, the most delicious steak dinner I could prepare—nothing would be appreciated as much as a positive and happy attitude.

My second rule as comforter to my family is: Let them know what my priorities are and *let them know they are first in my life.* How comforting it is to your husband or wife to hear again and again, "You are first in my life!" "You are more important to me than this job." "Honey, I love my career, but I want you to know you are more important to me and I love you far more."

No husband or wife *ever* outlives the need to hear these comforting words month after month, year after year.

And the children need to be comforted with these same words also: "You are more important than my career!"

These priorities still must remain important in the value system of a career wife and mother. I know some very, very successful career women who never stopped being *comforters* to their families by letting them know they came *first.* Because of their attitude, these women enjoy successful marriages and fantastic families, as well as more-than-million-dollar careers.

Recently, I attended a board meeting where a single girl in her early twenties was interviewing for an executive management role. I was saddened when she said: "Naturally, if I marry and have a family, I will put my career first."

I wanted to shake her and say, "No! No! Your value system is all upside down! Believe me, it is possible to succeed in all three areas, when the priorities are in the right order."

In being a comforter to my husband, I frequently need to ask myself the question, "What can I do that will comfort him?" It then becomes an adventure and joy to do many little chores for him, not out of duty, for then I would resent it, but out of love. Surely if I love him, the least I can do is to make him comfortable. The neat thing about this attitude is that I do not become a doormat for him, but rather he tries to get even with me and returns the favor by doing all kinds of nice little things that will make me comfortable.

I suppose you wonder what are some of the things we do for each other in the role of comforter. Now if I shared them with you, you just might react and say, "Why doesn't my husband do that for me?" or "Why doesn't my wife treat me like that?"

But here goes!

Very seldom do I have to pick up after my husband when he shaves or dresses. He is quick to offer his help with chauffeuring the children or getting some Colonel Sanders chicken if he sees I have had a busy day.

Meanwhile, I keep his wardrobe in order. Keeping in close touch with his secretary, I am aware of his daily calendar so I can hang out an appropriate suit and shirt with tie. I noticed many years ago that he didn't want to be bothered with the mundane decision about what to wear on the start of a new day. When he goes on an out-of-town trip, he seldom knows what I've packed for him, but again I consult his schedule and try to include what he needs. (It is always fun to pack a little love note in his shirt pocket, or better yet . . . in his underwear.)

One of the most beautiful ways in which my husband fulfilled his role as a comforter to me was after my mastec-

tomy just two weeks before my fiftieth birthday. Not only is it
difficult to deal with that dreaded diagnosis of cancer, but
then to get home and look at your lopsided self with ugly
scars in the mirror is a deflating experience. I had always
prided myself in keeping my figure attractive for my husband
—but now this? Many, many times he reassured me that it
made no difference, that he loved me for who I was, not for
my physical beauty, but I still struggled to believe him. I
bought lacy little cover-ups and camisoles that concealed my
scars.

The following Christmas, our family was eagerly preparing
for a two-week holiday in sunny Hawaii. Only I was not enthusiastic. What would I look like in a bathing suit? Would
the scars show? Would people stare at me? I shared some of
these concerns with Jeanne, our college-student daughter, just
home for the holidays. She sympathized with my fears and
apparently confided in my husband. Together they conspired
and went shopping the day before Christmas. On Christmas
morning I eagerly opened a little overnight suitcase to find inside not one but three different bathing suits with matching
cover-ups, all designed for women who had had mastec-
tomies.

Bob's beaming face watched my eyes fill with tears and I
knew that my husband's love was the most comforting force
in my world. How lucky I was to be his wife!

Gone is resentment, gone is the self-pity of "Who needs
me?" when we see each other in this positive unchanging role
of comforter. We all need to give, as well as receive, the mutual support that chases away fear.

THE COMPANION

When our family senses that we are each other's comforters, they will see the next unchanging role—that of companion. But a *helpful companion must first be a comforter.*

Who wants a companion that is negative, or nagging or "bugging" you? Who wants a companion who is never available or never has time for you? Sometimes the loneliest person in the world is the one who sleeps under your roof, or next to you in your bed.

New Year's resolutions are a must in our home. We make quite a production of sharing our New Year's goals with each other, for we have found that we have a stronger commitment to those goals and dreams that we dare to share aloud than to those we lack the courage to express.

Six years ago, sitting around the New Year's breakfast table, we took turns telling the other family members what we wanted to accomplish during the next year. When the spotlight settled on me, I quietly announced that I was concerned about the passing of time. The children were growing up too fast. Even though I had good intentions, I felt I was not spending enough in-depth time with our daughters. My goal for 1977, I announced, was to set aside one day each month for a special "date day" with each of my children. Furthermore, I resolved that if their grades averaged B or above, I would allow them to skip school in order to have the extra time that I knew this plan would require.

Their enthusiastic response overwhelmed me. They craved my sole attention as much as I yearned for a private time with each of them. To this day, I have not outlived this New Year's resolution; in fact, it became an instant tradition. When my two married children and Jeanne, who was in college, heard about it, they also asked to be included. Even now it is common for me to receive a telephone call from one of them saying, "Mom, it's time for my date day! What's your schedule like?"

A magic evolves from talking on a one-to-one basis, with no competition for attention from another family member. A mutual in-depth sharing of hopes, dreams, and fears eases loneliness and builds confidence and understanding. This precious experience becomes ours when we see ourselves in the positive roles of a companion to our family members.

Therefore my first rule for this role of companion is: *Be available!*

I learned this secret many years ago from another woman who made a lasting positive impression on my life: Mrs. Richard Neutra.

As a young aspiring musician in Austria, Dione fell in love and married a struggling young architect, Richard Neutra. Later she followed him to America, where, in California, he became known as a founder of the international style in architecture. My husband and I would work closely with him for eighteen years in planning and designing our church.

In her beautiful letters to us, Mrs. Neutra related how her husband, not being able to sleep at night, would often ask her to wake up, play the cello, and sing for him. This she did year after year, while mothering three children through sickness and health. As she sang and played in the dark of night a beautiful creative experience evolved. For Richard Neutra would begin to dream, then draw and design. How much he depended on her presence and her song, the assurance that she was there—available to him.

The last time we visited the Neutras before his death, Dione graciously served us a simple but elegant Austrian meal. We then climbed the stairs of the new Neutra-designed home so that we could see and catch the flowing lines of architecture which jutted out against the night sky.

Mrs. Neutra recognized the greatness in her husband long before the world saw and acknowledged his designs. Believing in him, she made herself available to him so that he could draw out inner potential that had hardly begun to surface. I have no doubt in my mind that, as a companion to her husband, Mrs. Neutra contributed enormously to his fame and success. Still she retained her musical abilities. Her husband quickly and proudly asked her to entertain his visiting clients.

Dione Neutra, now eighty, is one of few musicians who have mastered the difficult art of accompanying their own voices with contrapuntal melodies on the cello. Her concerts through the years have included art songs professionally performed in Italian, French, German, and English.

Be available. As a wife, I have really used this rule in my role as companion. For I know there are a lot of women out there who will gladly make themselves "available" for my husband. I've left dishes in the sink, laundry to be finished tomorrow. Numerous projects are still not completed, because I've chosen my husband as my first priority. To be his companion, I need to be available to him and for him.

Then, to be available for the family is second in importance. When Carol was twelve, she was in the girls' softball league. After the first team practice, she excitedly came home to tell me she had nominated me, her mom, to be an assistant to the manager of her team. Really complimented by her belief in me, I asked her what that really meant. Carol answered by pulling a list out of her pocket, informing me that I had to be at every practice and game, providing ice water, Styrofoam cups, lemonade, Band-Aids, hairpins, lots of motivation, and treats (in case they should win).

What a spring season we had—two games a week! Dozens of treats, skinned knees, and tearful girls later, I was grateful that Carol believed I would be available, for I had as much fun as she. Yes, we had many late dinners. Some were a real disaster, but Carol and I were enjoying a beautiful companionship.

A changing world is a hurting and lonely world unless we see each other as comforters and companions. Once we've become adjusted to these two roles, we automatically find ourselves taking on a third role, the role of counselor.

THE COUNSELOR

A changing world is also a confusing world, and so within the walls of a home, we need to be counselors to each other. Husbands counseling wives, wives counseling husbands, parents counseling children, and, yes, children giving counsel to parents.

"Wait a minute!" we say. "That's the problem with our family. We are always telling each other what to do!" The last thing we want to hear is that we need to be counseled, especially by members of our own family. If we can defuse our defense mechanisms, quit being rebellious and resentful, then we can fulfill the role of a counselor.

None of us can succeed as counselor if we ignore the first two requisites of being a positive and loving comforter and companion. I need to reemphasize the importance of the order of these roles. Without this order, we fall flat on our face in the unchanging role of counselor. And yet we desperately need the loving counsel of each other in the family. Being able to react wisely to each other keeps each of us from becoming a recluse, a reactionary, or an eccentric. This is the strength of the family. Where there is a positive, loving, caring atmosphere we keep each other from going off the deep end.

Usually without warning, I suddenly find myself acting as a counselor while chauffeuring Gretchen to a piano lesson or cooking supper. Or sometimes late at night, past my bedtime, one of our teens will bring up a problem he or she wants to talk through. What then are some of the rules I have for my role as counselor in our home?

Rule number one for the counselor is: *Be a good listener!* Most of us are just too busy to listen intently to our children and spouses. What are they really saying? Am I giving them a chance to express what they feel, where they hurt, or do I hear a few facts and then glance at the clock because I'm late for some appointment?

Our New Hope Suicide Prevention Twenty-four-Hour Telephone Center teaches its counselors to be very sensitive in recognizing the emotion of the voice of the caller. Is there fear? Anger? Loneliness? Desperation? Confusion in the tone of the voice? The reaction of the counselor to these emotions becomes crucial in a life-or-death situation. Also the counselor is taught that the tone of his or her own voice is telling and critical. Our voices change tone when we smile or frown as we speak on a telephone. A counselor's calm, confident, loving tone is as important as the reassuring words that he or she says. A wise counselor is one who says little but lets people talk themselves out. Often, they don't need any advice or counsel, for as they talk they answer their own questions. Solutions become obvious when the problems are verbalized in a comforting environment.

These same guidelines are necessary for the positive parent as he counsels the family. Sometimes I ask such questions as: What do you really think about this? Are you afraid of your feelings? Is this what you really want? What do *you* think you should do?

Most of the time the children will talk through all the sides of a problem and come to their own conclusions about what has to be done. With a look of contentment on their faces they will walk away from me saying, "Thanks, Mom." And I'm thankful I didn't give in to the temptation to interrupt with an "I-know-it-all" pat solution.

Rule number two for the counselor is: Always end a counseling moment with a compliment or a positive affirmation to your companion. Many times this is all that is needed to calm a troubled child, teen, or husband. We never outlive the need to be reassured that we are okay in the eyes of family members—brothers, sisters, husbands, wives, children, parents, young people.

Rule number three: Use the gift within you called "common sense." I don't know how to describe this gift, but I thank God for it. And it is the sixth sense that none of us can afford to ignore.

My husband often quotes one of his seminary professors: *"Use your head and your heart will follow!"* What wise advice. We often repeat this slogan to each other.

Common sense seems like such a boring and uninteresting theme, but what a vital ingredient in the home. Television, movies, books and songs encourage us to forget our common sense and chase rainbows to unrealistic relationships. Yes, we must always search and long for the romance in life, but not in disregard to plain old-fashioned common sense.

Rule number four: *Accept* the counsel of your children and your mate. What wise counsel they have for you. God only knows what mistakes I have been kept from making by sharing a decision-making problem with the family. Today I make few decisions (buying clothes, planning parties, critiquing church programs, decorating the home, etc.) in isolation, without the advice of the best decision making team of experts available to me—my family.

THE COMMITTOR

A changing world is a chaotic world when there is no abiding commitment to each other. If I may coin a word, we need to see ourselves as "committors"—to each other.

Why is insecurity the root cause of many of the problems that plague not only our families but all of society? I believe that the lack of commitment in relationships is the malignant cell that produces this devastating cancer.

"Till death us do part," what comforting words! They form a lifelong sense of security between husband and wife, which in turn creates an atmosphere of comfort and companionship, which in turn produces boundless creativity in setting goals and building dreams for the family as a unit as well as for the separate individuals.

"We, as a family, can solve *any* problem! Meet any crisis! No matter how great! We, as a family, will stick together!" Constantly we reaffirm each other.

"You will always be my son, even if I do not approve of your life-style."

"I will always be your mother—I will always be your father —for we have a 'love that will not quit.'"

Recently our college student came home for a brief Christmas vacation. She quickly found herself overwhelmed by the crush of holiday events, holiday shopping, friends calling and visiting, and, on top of it all, a term paper to complete before her return to class. Sensing that she was overwhelmed, I came to her aid by offering to launder her clothes. It seemed like such a small thing, but she reacted with grateful spirit, for she knew that my calendar was overscheduled also. With tear-filled eyes, she thanked me for "your love that will not quit!" Perhaps she had been away from the atmosphere of our home long enough to notice that this type of committed love is extraordinary and rare. How necessary for each of us in a family circle to sense and then remind one another of the depth of our relationship. *We will not quit on each other.* As we build secure and healthy emotions an immeasurable happiness will overwhelm us.

No matter how absurd life around us may seem, we must not lose sight of these four universal, unchangeable roles: we all must be and have comforters, companions, counselors, and committors. If those four roles remain constant, we need not fear changes in other "traditional roles."

THE CAPTIVATED HUSBAND
AND THE LIBERATED WIFE

In August of 1977, our family was vacationing for a few days at our mountain cabin. But for me, it was a working vacation. I became engrossed in meeting a programming deadline for the fall season of our television program. I ignored everything else, as I desperately wanted to complete my paperwork.

It was about 5 P.M. and the breakfast dishes were still soaking in the sink. My husband, with our daughters Carol and Gretchen, came in from fishing.

With one quick glance at the situation, Bob knew he would have to pitch in and be responsible not only for doing the dishes but also for cooking up some food for four hungry people.

A born leader and organizer, he quickly recruited and organized the girls into KP duty. With his motivating expertise, the three dishwashers and driers sprang to action. They all joined in a hearty chorus, teasing me about the changed husband and wife roles. Here I sat with piles of notes around me, and there was Bob, with an apron tied around his waist, arms up to his elbows in suds.

Minutes later, amid giggles of laughter, the lyrics of a song began to emerge. When the dishwashing came to an end, Bob picked up the guitar and with the help of Gretchen and Carol composed these amusing lines:

I am the captivated husband of a liberated wife,
Marriage to an executive has surely changed my life.
Once had lots of lovin'—now all I have is strife,
'Cause I'm the captivated husband to a liberated wife.

She goes to work each morning—drives the biggest car,
She's climbin' up the ladder—goin' very far,
Sits behind her office desk, in a fancy downtown store,
I'm alone with daytime TV—quickly that's a bore.

In fancy clothes, she leaves the house—kisses me goodbye,
Goes to lunch in restaurants, high up in the sky.
She's left me with the house and yard, the dog, and all the
      kids,
I do all the washing—pots and pans and lids.

She brings home the money—and a "Honey, how are you?"
I tell her, "Thanks," and smile, but in my heart I'm blue.
I plan to make her happy with a special meal,
"Sorry, dear, I'm tired tonight—food has no appeal."

She feels like a million—I feel like a mouse,
She has got the power, I have got the house.
Once I knew she needed me but that's not true today,
So how can I keep lovin' her along this changin' way?

REFRAIN:
I am the captivated husband of a liberated wife,
Marriage to an executive has surely changed my life.
Once had lots of lovin'—now all I have is strife,
'Cause I'm the captivated husband to a liberated wife.*

I don't remember what we ate for supper that night, but it
was a creative end to a beautiful day, and we realized that
our changing roles would find us together—no matter what!

* Copyright 1977 by Robert H. Schuller.

4

POSITIVE COMMUNICATION THROUGH A LOOK, A WORD, AND A TOUCH

"All I really want from my family is to have them *treat me like they treat our poodle.*"

"What do you mean?" My husband was shocked at this distraught woman's admission. She sat across from his desk and poured out a frustrated story of discontentment concerning her husband and children.

"All I want is *a look, a word, a touch!* When my husband or kids come home, they always take time to notice Jo Jo, our poodle! They notice her, they call her by name, and give her a loving pat! She is important to them!"

"A look, a word—a touch"—this woman in one simple sentence stated the essence of all communication. Volumes have been written and spoken on this subject, and still, in the most intimate relationships, communication is the area where success comes hard and failure easy and often. Yet it is a most important ingredient in all of family relationships—husband-and-wife or parent-and-child.

Communication does not just automatically happen in a

COMMUNICATION THROUGH A LOOK, A WORD, A TOUCH

family—especially not today, when all kinds of interruptions and intrusions on our privacy complicate the communications between one another. When we close the door to our home, we are no longer shutting out the rest of the world.

The largest obstacle to communication in modern homes may well be the television set. It dominates the life-style of entire families. It has become an easy tool for achieving family peace and quietness. "Go watch TV" often ends a quarrel or puts a stop to a young child's constant interruptions.

Television contributes to breakdowns in family communication when it gives a *distorted* image to marriage and family life.

The December 14, 1981, issue of *U.S. News & World Report* stated that one million teens between the ages of fifteen and nineteen become pregnant each year, out of wedlock. A seventeen-year-old high school girl observed, "If your sexual life isn't like Luke and Laura's on 'General Hospital,' you ain't got it."

Communication within the home has also been hampered by the overwhelming barrage of automatic appliances that need only one individual to operate them. Add on the noise factor and gone is the talking, laughing, and listening that used to be such an important part of washing dishes, or raking leaves, or carrying the garbage out. Now, one person pushes a button and the automatic noise that follows drowns out important communication that would be taking place if two people were working side by side. When sharing efforts to get a job done, one's defensive barriers often break down. Listening becomes easier and somehow a stage is magically set for effective and long-reaching communication.

So much of my mother's wise counsel came to me when we did dishes together (washing and drying dishes for a family of nine takes a long time), when we did the laundry together (hanging clothes on a clothesline), or when we washed windows or walls together. Not once when I was a child or teen did my mother say, "Come, Arvella, it's time we had a talk!" Never once did she say, "Sit here with me, I need to have a long talk with you!" It wasn't necessary and I wonder now if I would have listened. I learned of sex, boys, God, work—life—as I worked side by side with my parents. And I learned how to give and take when I was assigned to work side by side with brothers and sisters.

I thoroughly enjoy the times Bob, the children, and I spend in our mountain cabin, where there are no "automatics." Everyone takes his or her turn at dishes and preparing meals. What a joy to listen to the impromptu creative communication.

Because many of these family communication times no longer exist, it is most essential—in fact, a death-or-life situation—for families to program times, places, and feelings that will replace this vacuum. How often we have heard a husband or a wife, parent, or teen say, "All we do is yell at each other; we just can't seem to communicate anymore."

Husbands and wives that COMMUNICATE regularly stay together, and families that COMMUNICATE on a regular basis have successful and meaningful relationships.

A POSITIVE LOOK

Let's begin with the first of the three simple steps to communication: a positive look.

When we see someone day in and day out for years on end, we don't notice changes that occur slowly. We get used to each other and are surprised at the obvious. We wake up and say, "How quickly the children have grown," or "I didn't notice how tired he was," or "My, she really is gray," or "I hadn't noticed that he really has put a spare tire around his waist."

How important the appearance of our partners was when we were dating. That "adoring" look often disappears after marriage or, worse yet, sometimes it is replaced with a critical look. The attentive look is so important in healthy communications. Take time each day to look at your partner. Is her face more beautiful now than it was five years ago? Is his face strong but gentle? Does he show fatigue lines? Are her eyes alive and exciting?

Be sensitive about when you choose to say, "Why not try a new hairdo?" or "Let me buy you something new for your wardrobe!" A quiet setting and a calm atmosphere where you can enjoy looking at each other in depth makes constructive criticism much easier to accept than when you are rushing out to a PTA meeting to present the ways-and-means report. At that time the critical look of a partner can devastate one's confidence. "If looks could kill . . ." Parents and partners learn quickly that the facial expressions of family members communicate approval or disapproval loudly and clearly.

When there is no time for talk, we must learn quickly the all-important lesson that a positive look, and I-am-proud-of-you look, can make or break a day.

One morning recently, as Bob was leaving for work, he stopped just inside the front door. He turned to fifteen-year-old Carol and said, "Carol, you are pretty. I love you and want you to know that I trust you completely. I know who your Lord is." This eye-to-eye, soul-to-soul exchange made Carol beam with a rainbow of joy. She knew by the look on his face that he was proud of her.

"*All I want is a look*." Husbands, wives, children, and our world all cry out for this wordless in-depth communication. For the inner soul through the eyes speaks the most beautiful words of love.

I learned early to read the innermost thoughts of my children by looking at their faces. How well do you know your family?

I have seen fear, determination, pain, guilt, love, hate, resentment, joy, anger—all of the emotions—displayed at various times. When too much of a negative emotion continues to show, it is time to take a serious long look at a child's friends, habits, regular television programs, yes, even in his room or his favorite and private desk drawer.

One of the most meaningful experiences a parent can have

is to lie down on his or her child's bed. We do this often. Flat on our back, we look up at the ceiling and take a good look at the same sight our teen or child sees when he is scared or angry. There is a hangup today about the privacy of our children's rooms and I sense an overreaction of many parents who feel guilty or "snoopy" in rummaging through a child's room. I agree wholeheartedly that each child needs a private place that is all his own, but I also sense that this can lead to serious problems if parents misunderstand the meaning of a child's privacy.

Ideally, parents and children or parents and teens clean, sort, and rearrange drawers together. It makes for a fascinating all-day experience.

"Why are you saving this dried-up corsage?" or "You may not see that letter, Mom, that's private!" Why do your children collect the things they do?

I submit that it is absolutely necessary for responsible parents to know what contents are a part of our children's private world. How else will we really continue to know what their innermost thoughts are?

To become acquainted with your child's private room or drawer is absolutely necessary for you and me to be knowledgeable and therefore better parents. This, then, is the positive reason for a positive look at your child. Not a suspicious or investigating or worried or negative look, but a positive look with your child at his most private surroundings allows you to understand him and know where he is at.

I grew up in a tradition where spring and fall housecleaning was a must. So this is an exercise that I continued after I established my own home and family. One of the chores connected to this tradition was to religiously, twice a year, turn the mattresses on the beds.

One morning, I asked my husband to help me turn the mattress on our eleven-year-old son's bed. Young Bobby was already at school, and my husband and I were both shocked and surprised to find a popular magazine about sex tucked between the mattress and spring of our son's bed. My husband's reaction was immediately positive: "Well, at least we know he is a healthy, normal, growing boy!" And we both knew it was time to share with him more about the birds and bees. That night an embarrassed boy shared how he found such magazines in a garbage can in the alley on his way home from school. We, as parents, grateful that we knew what his interests were, could now better guide his curiosity toward positive avenues in his growing up. A positive look at our children's private world is a beautiful experience, and when this is done in a respectful attitude, we become better parents giving wiser advice. Take a good look around his or her room and get into your child's world.

We have taught our family to look each other directly in the eye. I was most impressed by one of the first rules I heard my husband share: "I will not hire any person who does not look me squarely in the eyes." This rule is carried over into our family. When we reprimand or when we talk of love, we say, "Look at me! I love you very much!" or "Look at me! Tell me why you did that!" Direct eye contact establishes the fact that we are sincere and that we expect honesty and sincerity in return.

I shall long remember Dad Schuller's amazing ability to speak with his eyes. He was a reserved person but he had the gift of being able to sit in a large room filled with his married sons and daughters and grandchildren of all ages, and without saying a word he would exude a joy, love, and contentment that was infectious. He was truly a man of few words, but his eyes and face assured us of his love.

In the September 1977 issue of *Reader's Digest*, I read of one woman's reason for her happy, fifty-year-old marriage. She said, "Early in our marriage, we learned to see through each other . . . and still enjoy the view!" What a beautiful testimony to the power of the unspoken word.

Some years ago we had a lovely babysitter who was totally deaf. Our children were old enough to answer the telephone, so we felt this was a great experience for all of us to learn to communicate without talking. Kathy remained our sitter until she married. Today she is the excited young mother of an active little toddler. Kathy, her family, and now her husband have learned the art of silent communication. How very important this first step of communication really is: *"All I want is a look."*

A POSITIVE WORD

We talk, talk, talk, talk, and yet there seems so much we don't know how to say. Is it because the fast talk that accompanies the fast food and instant breakfasts is not adequate for all the communication needed to keep the family wheels running smoothly?

For many years, we had a family rule: No student in high school could elect the very early morning classes. We wanted to preserve our family breakfasts together. It was rough at times to gather five days a week—Monday through Friday—around the kitchen table, but we managed. We *needed* those minutes together. At 7:30 A.M. the family would rush to the table for their meal—cold cereal, toast and table talk. "I've got practice after school today!" "Pray for me at eleven this morning; I'll be taking an algebra exam that's going to be murder." "Mom, do I have to go to school today? The kids are so mean to me."

Only fifteen minutes together, but it got us talking and it helped us think of each other's needs throughout the day.

One of the sad statistics of our society is that family dinners at home are fast disappearing. Kids eat on the run; fathers and mothers arrive home late from work and eat in front of the television or while reading the mail or newspaper; a quick bite from a fast-food store does the trick.

I can't begin to measure the success of our family without paying tribute to the great times we regularly experienced around the table at dinner. The food isn't always the greatest, but dinner is an event to be savored.

The TV is turned off! Hands are washed and appropriate clothes are put on (no swimming-suit or shirtless diners are allowed), the candles are lit—even for "Schuller Spaghetti." A runner is appointed to answer the telephone and also get any forgotten dinner items such as salt and pepper. We even use cloth napkins. There are such great wash-and-wear ones on the market now and we each have our own labeled napkin ring. (The trick is to reward those who keep their napkins cleanest for the longest period of time—perhaps even one week.)

Why such a production? It is a stage set for relaxed communication without interruption. If the telephone rings, our runner takes a message. He or she informs the caller that we are eating dinner and assures that the call will be returned when we finish (emergencies, naturally, excepted). Oftentimes Bob will clear the table and serve the dessert. Having worked as a waiter during college years, he puts on his "act," bending at the waist, dusting off a glass, serving "Madam" or "M'sieur." Through the years the children thoroughly enjoy this special treatment.

If no one is talking, Bob or I quickly lead the conversation with, "Okay what is the best and worst that happened to you today?" Or "What did you learn today that you never knew before?"

Our family is clearly divided between the talkers and the nontalkers, so we are sensitive to the quiet ones, drawing them out.

Yes, there are disasters at the family table. At times a rule is broken, and some teasing will start, sibling criticism will mount, or even a wing-ding argument will flare up. Sometimes someone will jump up and head for his or her room, but before the meal is over and the family is dismissed, we join again around the table. Apologies are made and accepted. Peace is established.

Naturally, because we are a Christian family, devotions are

a part of our meals—both breakfast and dinner. We take turns in sharing prayers and reading the Bible. If one of the children is particularly eager to share something, we will sit a little longer and listen to her after the others are dismissed.

Our goal, then, is for daily mealtime talking. Yes, there are days when we grab a hamburger on the run. But we notice that all sorts of irritations and crises arise when we miss our daily table talk together.

Then there must be a program for *in-depth* talking with the family, and so it has become my assignment to calendar "vacations" designed for communicating. Because my husband and I have such busy weekends in our work, planning family weekend times is difficult. Therefore, it is extremely important that I look a year in advance to schedule family weekends when a school holiday does not compete with my husband's schedule. As soon as I know these holidays, they are programmed on our calendars as commitments.

As important as the *time* on the calendar is the *place* where this communication happens. Each family knows *where* it can be most relaxed—at the beach, traveling in a car or mobile home, in a tent in the desert. For over ten years our place has been a mountain cabin that we planned and built. For many years there was no clock, no calendar, no telephone, radio, or television. There was little to do except take long hikes in the woods, go on a picnic, or spend long hours fishing at the lake.

Bobby was never listed among the talkers in our family, and as he became a teenager he talked less and less. If I asked him, "How is school?" the answer would be "Okay." End of conversation. However, soon after we arrived at the cabin, a new and different Bobby emerged. There was something about the atmosphere or the setting that released the cork of his inner spirit. As the rest of the family would retreat one by one to bed, an energetic Bobby began to share and discuss first just some tidbits here and there, then deep and studious questions and comments. As the hours approached midnight, 1 A.M., 2 A.M.—Bobby continued to talk, talk, talk, talk.

Perhaps he knew he had his parents all to himself now—no interruptions from work or neighbors—while at the same time his world was not pressuring him for his attention. It was a great relief for us, as parents, to have these times together when we could know our son's deepest feelings. How important this was not only for our parent-child relationship, but also for his development.

If your child is not sharing or talking, perhaps the place is not right, the atmosphere might be too restrictive, or the time is not right. Talking—a word—is a vital part of effective communication.

One night on our way out to "date night," as Bob and I said our goodbyes to the children, Carol, who was then eleven, said, "How come you and Daddy always date, and I don't get to date Daddy?"

Bob and I looked at each other and immediately got the signal: Carol wanted Daddy all to herself and she wanted it to be special. "Okay," we said, "tomorrow we will look at Daddy's calendar and find a night when you and he can have a date time." The following Thursday, Carol spent all of her after-school hours getting dressed up for dinner—out with Daddy. With her hair brushed, and wearing her best dress, she watched the clock, ready for Daddy to come home from work. What a wonderful evening they had! Since that time, whenever we sense that our kids need Dad all to themselves, we arrange a "Dad date time" in the calendar. It can be a breakfast, lunch, or dinner. And once a year a fishing trip overnight for father and son—a talk . . . a word . . . we all need that.

Children are asking for parents to listen. They have things they want to share. It's fun to get into their world, it really is. I can forget my little problems when I live in their world, with them.

Then I also communicate with them at bedtime. I hear their prayers and again talk alone with them. As a young mother, I was impressed and influenced by the example of Suzanna Wesley, a devout English mother of sixteen children,

who made it her practice to spend twenty minutes each week
alone with each child. I immediately questioned, "How could
she possibly have found the time?" Sixteen children—no automatic washer and dryer or electric kitchen. Two of her sons
became great religious leaders of the eighteenth century, leaving the world a rich heritage of beautiful poetic verse. If she
could find time to have a look, a word, a touch with each of
her children in eighteenth-century England, I could find the
time to have this kind of a relationship with my five children
in our bustling, active twentieth-century automatic all-
American home.

I remember the night I went in to say good night to our
eighteen-year-old. "Mom, will you come in and pray with me?
This will be my last night at home," was her simple request.
Our children have all gained great strength and closeness to
us as we spend time quietly in prayer and just talking alone
with them. Kids need to hear their parents tell them over and
over again, "I love you," "I'm proud of you," "I'll back you all
the way!"

A POSITIVE TOUCH

Without a look, without a word, the touch isn't very
significant. There is a great deal written by psychiatrists and
psychologists on the therapy of the touch. It is hard to
overemphasize the tremendous importance of the loving
touch.

Two weeks ago I stood at the entrance of an intensive care
unit for newborn babies. I had picked up my husband from
the airport and had driven him directly to this hospital, which
has one of the best such care units in our nation. And I took
him there for one purpose: my husband was to administer the
sacrament of baptism to a tiny six-hour-old baby who was not
expected to survive. We were to meet the father right outside the entrance of the ICU.

Through the glass walls, I watched my husband wash his hands, put on a gown and then the plastic gloves, and enter the unit. As I waited, I observed probably fifteen babies, some weighing no more than two pounds, most of them in incubators. All of them had tubes coming out of their tiny little nostrils. Some had tubes coming out of their little abdomens, having just had surgery. These babies were struggling for survival. There was an attendant—a trained nurse—at nearly every baby's side. Each nurse appeared to be constantly talking, calling "her baby" by name. She would *touch* the baby while she watched all the meters and the gauges of the instruments. A look, a word, a touch, was a most necessary procedure for the survival of these infants. Is it not as necessary for you and me and our children to have this look, this word, this touch, constantly in order to survive in our world?

In 1972, I accompanied my husband and two college-age children on a semester-at-sea South Pacific college cruise. Bob filled the role of professor of religion and college chaplain.

I enrolled in the anthropology course on board, and was deeply excited to be studying the cultures and peoples of the South Sea islands and the Orient, observing firsthand what we had learned in textbooks.

When the ship arrived in port at Papua, New Guinea, the four of us flew, along with our class, in to Mt. Hagen in the highlands of that island. Today there are American hotels that serve the tourists, but then there was only a brand-new airstrip, a youth hostel, and a mission compound to accommodate our needs. For two nights and three days we traveled by trucks and jeep over rivers and trails to villages only a generation removed from cannibalism. The sound of our engine attracted the village people out of the jungles and bush. We came to look at them; they came to stare at us. The females wore no clothes with the exception of small loin cloths made of grass leaves, while the males wore gourds to cover their genitals. Smelling of pig grease, which they rubbed over their bodies to keep insects off and to stay warm, they came near us. They wanted to touch our white faces. The oldest women were only fortyish, while the young mothers were twelve and thirteen years old.

We were cautioned to be friendly, to smile continually, and to give gifts of jewelry or shiny articles.

I was impressed how the young mothers carried their babies. Bare skin against bare skin, often the baby's hands grasping the mother's breast. There was much we American mothers had that they didn't have, but they had an essential ingredient to human communication—the touch.

About seven years ago we moved to a new area in our community, which meant that the children changed school districts in the middle of the year. Our daughter Jeanne, who was in her sophomore year in high school, had been with her friends since kindergarten. I knew that this would be a traumatic move for her, and I became concerned about it. My fears were justified. When she started going to her new school I knew that she was without friends, eating her lunches alone. It was difficult for her to make new friends.

I watched her withdraw from her usually happy, outgoing self to an irritable, unhappy person. Whenever she spoke to us it was with a sharp tongue. As November turned to December, I became more and more concerned for her. One school morning I went into her room to awaken her. Instead of just knocking on the door and saying my usual "Jeanne. Time for school. Come on. Let's get up." I went in and I sat on her bed, but said nothing for a while. I began to stroke her hair. Then, still silent, I just sat stroking her. After a few minutes I began talking in a quiet voice. I said things like "Jeanne, it's about time for school. I'm so glad God made you the way you are. Jeanne, you're growing up to be so pretty. If I were God I wouldn't want to change anything about the way you're made. Your long auburn hair, your beautiful eyes. I know God's got a great plan for your life. You're born for a purpose, I can see that." I kept this up every day for several weeks, and a transformation came over her. Her own normal outgoing, happy self returned with the therapy of touch, which all of us need. Your teen children need it. Your young children need it, and you and I need it.

I shall never forget one of our Institutes for Successful Leadership. A reserved Dutch minister from the Midwest shared how he and his twenty-year-old son were on the outs with each other. They didn't agree on anything, and the rift hurt him deeply. In the same discussion group sat a friend of ours, the manager of a small Italian restaurant that we frequent for a favorite supper of spaghetti. Italians are known as exuberant, affectionate, outgoing people, and Eddie fit the stereotype perfectly. There came a time in this small group discussion when the pastor broke down and began to cry about the nonexistent relationship between him and his son. Eddie thought the solution was obvious, "Well, why don't you just hug him? Why don't you give him a big bear hug? I do that with my papa all the time."

Teenagers, adolescents, tiny children, husbands and wives, parents and children—all are begging for positive loving communication. "Look at me. Look and see what I'm really like."

"Get to know me. Speak to me. I need somebody to talk to."

"Won't you touch me, hold me? Let me feel the love flow from you to me."

The basic problem with the American family today is that . . . We've stopped looking! We've stopped talking! We've stopped touching! If we are to heal the hurts of our nation, let's begin with the family.

5

HAPPINESS IS BEING MARRIED

A good marriage makes a successful family so much easier.

Some time ago I found myself at a luncheon seated next to a young psychologist who specialized in marriage counseling.

"Tell me," I questioned, "what are the most common problems you encounter in your patients?" I expected there would be quite a list, perhaps beginning with the problem of alcoholism, followed by a close second of "another man or woman," then quarreling over money and children.

I was taken aback by his immediate and quick response. "That's an easy one to answer! All of the problems in marriage fall into two categories: *SELFISHNESS* and/or *IMMATURITY!*"

I looked at this professional expert with surprise and respect. As I flashed back on the disagreements in my marriage of over twenty years I silently admitted that both selfishness and immaturity on the part of me or my husband (or both) would correctly diagnose the cause behind the tension times in my marriage too. But I questioned again. "Am I hearing you correctly? Are you saying that you would categorize an alcohol problem or a third person involvement so simply?"

"Yes," was his immediate reply. "The bottom line in all marriage failure is selfishness or immaturity."

He went on to explain that these two negative characteristics take on many different forms of expression.

The I-want-what-I-want-when-I-want-it attitude will destroy a marriage before it has a chance to develop into the beautiful intimate relationship of "oneness" that marriage is designed for.

For many years I have given a silver dressing spoon as a special wedding gift to close friends of the family. Accompanying the gift was a card with the wise saying expressed over two thousand years ago: "Give and you shall receive. Give in good measure shaken together, running over, pressed down; *for the measure you give is the measure you shall receive.*" In all of life, when the emphasis is on the "giving" instead of the "getting," something magic happens, and in no area is this philosophy more important or practical than in the marriage relationship. "Takers are losers and givers are winners" is certainly true in the arena we call marriage.

Often someone who is unhappy in marriage will remark to me, "Why do I always have to be the one to do the giving? I'm tired of always giving. I deserve to enjoy the getting once in a while instead of giving." There is a mystical phenomenon that happens when our focus shifts from *giving* (which we delighted in in those first days of courtship and marriage) to the *getting* attitude. The sweet springs of joy are polluted with a stream of negative emotions, sprinkling a staining rain upon the family and the community.

In a leading newspaper from Great Britain last year, I read about Britain's longest married couple. Mr. John Orton, 104, and his wife Harriet, 102, celebrated their eightieth wedding anniversary. When he was younger, he worked sixteen hours a day as a farmer. He said, "We had no time to quarrel. We fetched water from a river six miles away and made the hay with scythes." They credited their happiness to "hard work, *give* and *take*" and as devout Methodists credited "a lot of help from the good Lord above!"

"Love isn't put in your heart to stay . . . Love isn't love until you give it away" are the wise words carefully stitched in a fabric wall hanging in our dining room. It has helped—I am sure—shape the scene around many a family mealtime together.

Real love in a beautiful marriage relationship will release possibility thinking. Imagine the joys of the unfolding years of marriage! Then you'll be motivated to maturity and not let "little irritations" wreak havoc.

A dear friend confided many years ago that it was the little things that nearly destroyed her marriage. She related a horrible scene that was born out of a disagreement about the correct way to hang a roll of toilet paper. Should the paper unwind from the bottom of the roll or the top? Immature?

Then I shared with her that one of our first little quarrels (which was repeated more than once) happened when I would leave the cap off the toothpaste. It was some months before we both matured enough so that this issue no longer ruined entire days. Meanwhile I learned to be more sensitive to my husband's feelings and realized that if something really bugged him, I should try *not* to annoy him.

Take the long look: Ten years later the toothpaste episodes were unimportant. A workable solution had been found. When our budget became more relaxed, I simply purchased two tubes of toothpaste and to this day—thirty years later—we each have our private tube of toothpaste.

This past summer our family were guests at a home in Kashmir, in the remote mountain area of northern India. Our hostess greeted us with unusual charm and graciousness. Dressed in a beautiful blue sari of India silk, she ushered us into the sitting room of their home. During the course of the evening she shared many interesting facts about her life. Her husband, very successful in business, was traveling and away from home much of the time. She began to comment on the sad impressions of American families and married life that she had received mostly through magazines. (There was no

TV or radio in her home, but *Time* and *Newsweek* magazines were read with great interest.)

This lovely hostess shared how she and her husband enjoyed a happy marriage of twenty years, with two grown sons now in the University. She was quick to share her philosophy of success.

At age eighteen she was invited to her cousin's home, unaware that a man ten years older than she, also a guest, was in search of a wife, and was "looking her over."

The next day she was quite surprised to hear of the announcement of her engagement to this stranger and two weeks later the arranged marriage became official. In her own words, she shared how, for her, there had been no alternative but to make her marriage work. Since she had no other choice, all of her thoughts were directed toward the making of a successful marriage and home. She concluded her quick and confident summary of marriage with an exceptional use of the English language. "So there was much give and take, and marriages in America would be happier too, if there was no other alternative." I was reminded that the secret of a successful marriage is commitment. And commitment means to eliminate all negative alternatives and discharge all negative options until your only choice is the challenge to succeed.

Listening attentively to her mature understanding of marriage, I heard again the words in the traditional marriage ceremony—those words I had promised so many years ago. "*Will* you love him?" (Not *do* you love him?) Love always needs to be in the "becoming" stage—not stagnant, for then it quickly dies. Love must be constantly growing into a more precious, vibrant and abundant relationship. Love is a progressive act not a passive pact.

How then do some couples continue to love each other more? How do they grow more fascinated with each other emotionally and physically? Some of the practical suggestions that we have learned from others and use ourselves we share with you gladly.

NEVER STOP DATING EACH OTHER!

We were married approximately six years and our children were aged five and two. It was difficult to stretch our budget so that there would not be too much month for our money. More than that, there seemed to be so little time for private conversation and enjoyment of each other without interruptions from the children or—even worse—the telephone or doorbell. What made our home even less private was the fact that the office was also at home, so there were constant interruptions and virtually no privacy for family life.

The need for my husband and me to be together alone became acute when in the summer of 1956 a couple of college coeds lived with us for a number of weeks. Six people living together in a tiny, tiny house where we couldn't get away from each other proved too much for us and so one night my husband announced firmly and loudly to all, that he was taking me out on a date. When everyone responded, "What's the occasion?" he simply remarked, "I need to talk quietly with my wife. I love you all, but I love her more and want to spend a quiet evening alone with her."

We both enjoyed our "date" so much that we spontaneously agreed to make this a regular event on the calendar. We decided to set aside every Monday night for the rest of our lives. Why Monday? Because my husband's pressure day is Sunday. Monday to a minister is like Saturday to most workers. That was over twenty-five years ago when we set Monday nights aside.

And we have never yet outgrown the need to escape from the unavoidable interruptions in our household. We need to be away from the children saying, "Mom, pass the milk" or "Dad, can I have some more soup?" We need to get away from the telephone, the doorbell, or work that calls for our attention.

My husband has always paid for our night out from his

extra speaking income, but the babysitting was always paid out of my grocery money.

Usually we go out to dinner, but often, when we had little money, we would go to the beach and find a quiet place to be alone together or we would stop for an ice cream cone and "park" somewhere—to talk, that is!

Never do we double-date on our special night together. There are just the two of us. It's so much fun just to have each other all to ourselves! Good marriages just don't happen, we need to make them happen!

Our regularly scheduled date night put the two of us more at ease with each other during the remainder of the week. We don't have to interrupt each other's projects or work with little problems; we both know "date night talk time" is coming up. Very seldom is it such an emergency that it can't wait until our special night. This releases the two of us from unnecessarily nagging each other and gives tremendous freedom to each other's schedules.

It is hard to imagine what our marriage would be like today if we had not had our twenty-four years of weekly date nights—over twelve hundred nights together that we have purposely scheduled. There have been precious times of quietly holding hands—looking long into each other's eyes. First we talk "shop" in the beginning of the evening, often planning schedules for the family, discussing at length a concern for the attitudes or behavior of one of the children. We have discussed our budget and cash flow. We talk sometimes with such intensity that we are unaware of others watching us reach a compromise on "cash flow" or disciplining the children. We even get into deep philosophical discussions and our weekly night out really allows us to begin to know each other with a greater depth of understanding.

Because we are changing persons in a changing world, we are constantly becoming reacquainted with each other. So we have grown together—not apart—as the years have passed. How stimulating and interesting these nights are to both of us! Yes, there are times when one of us is very fatigued, but then he or she draws energy from the other. There is sometimes boredom with each other so we realize that we need to be stimulated by either a change of scenery or entertainment of some kind, but 95 percent of the time we want to just be together to cherish our talking and touching.

So often families have problems because they try to solve a major crisis with one or two statements, oftentimes with one or two negative remarks, as one of the family members goes out the door. That's *not* the time or the occasion to communicate any great truth or piece of wisdom. That *is* the time to say, "I care about you! I love you! I'm not sure I can agree with what you are doing, so let's talk about it at dinner tonight."

It is important that we always treat our weekly date time as a special occasion—an "event," if you please. This means that we look forward in anticipation to our "date" by looking our very best—dressing to please each other, making the evening a romantic celebration.

A doctor friend of ours shared with us the excitement of his marriage, telling us with great enthusiasm that through the years he and his wife have a daily habit of "breakfast out" together. He leaves home in the wee hours of the morning to prepare for surgery, and meanwhile she gets the children off to school. About nine or ten in the morning, when he is free, they meet for breakfast—their "talking time." I'm sure that there are frequent times when their work or circumstances are such that they can't keep their breakfast date, but we could tell from the enthusiasm of this handsome doctor for his wife of over twenty-five years that this commitment to each other was a high priority in his system of values, and it was more than effective in his marriage relationship.

After our daughter's accident in 1978, we found our lifestyle changed drastically for many months, and my husband and I found "breakfast out" together a tremendous need-filling experience that allowed us the courage to meet the day's difficulties. Today the two of us continue to eat breakfast out often—especially if our days are long and the pressures demanding.

If there is no talking in the kitchen, there will soon be less sexual happiness in the bedroom, and if there is boredom in the bedroom there is a restraint in the communication and sharing in the kitchen. I contend that one affects the other so completely that both areas of the marriage relationship need to be stimulated constantly.

THE SEX-CESSFUL MARRIAGE

One of the most difficult assignments in my life came one morning when a friend, Dr. William Banowsky of Pepperdine University in Los Angeles, telephoned and asked me to appear on his half-hour Saturday television program. He went on to explain that his guest was an author promoting freedom of sex. She was advocating that marriage was a frustrating force in sexual freedom and she was teaching this to youngsters of twelve and thirteen. I was not accustomed to appearing before television cameras and much less experienced in debate. However, I did know that I was tremendously excited about my marriage and my sexual happiness and fulfillment in it. Feeling a keen sense of responsibility to young couples who still believed that marriage offered the most beautiful of all relationships, I consented to appear.

My opponent was a beautiful French model—as articulate as she was beautiful. When I saw her, I felt I was outmatched. I listened carefully to glowing reports of her "happy" sexual experiences outside of marriage. Then I saw her weak point. Her sexual fulfillment was limited to the physical dimension. Quietly, I interrupted her. "I feel sorry for you," I said. "I sense that you will never experience the depth of sexual happiness I have found, for *physical* oneness is only the first step. Sexual happiness increases as a man and woman grow into oneness not only physically but *emo-*

tionally, intellectually, socially, and *spiritually.* To separate sexual fulfillment from these parts of your being is to experience only the shallowest sensation of sexuality. We were all designed to experience sex at a much higher level, but this is only possible when you and your partner are completely one in the other areas of your relationship."

Becoming caught up in my excitement, I continued: "You cannot separate or ignore the social, emotional, intellectual, and spiritual, as they are all interwoven into the sexual experience. Therefore, I do not believe it is possible to attain this oneness outside of a lifetime commitment. My husband and I enjoy each other *more* as the years go by. And because we share the same deep spiritual faith, our oneness has a *spirituality* that transends the *physical.*"

She gazed at me, stunned, and I knew that she realized she had settled for merely a shallow plastic satisfaction, not the precious and priceless gem that the Creator designed as the sexual union.

How sad that so many settle for the cheap imitation so widely advertised and exploited, and thereby are cheated from this priceless discovery of love transcending all boundaries of emotional, social, intellectual, physical, and spiritual limits.

"But even between committed lovers sex-cessful marriages don't just happen."

One wise counselor said that the marriage relationship goes into the doldrums about every five years, that the fifth year, the tenth, and the twentieth are the most shaky. *Stagnant relationships quickly become stale unless there is a stimulation.*

Stale marriage relationships are not only a twentieth-century ailment, for in the ancient Orient, many remedies were prescribed for sexual stimulation. The best known of these sexual stimulants was the practice of bound feet in China. From about 926 until 1911, women's feet were bound because "they were not only pleasing to the eye but also delightful to fondle."

The first bra in history was also introduced by these ancient lovemakers. To prevent love bites, one woman covered her breasts with a mini-apron. The delighted emperor believed she dressed this way to increase his desires and so the bra came into style.

Many foods, herbs, and wines were used to increase sexual pleasure; shadowboxing and meditation were also taught, to control correct breathing and willpower, so essential to achieving a joyous sexual performance.

Women ate a mixture of peonies, jasmine, magnolia, and other scented flowers in order to perfume their skin and breath. Some attached musical bracelets to wrists and ankles during lovemaking which greatly delighted the men.

Perhaps we should learn from these wise lovemakers how to stimulate each other in our bath and bedrooms.

There is no excuse for stagnating when all around us there are opportunities to grow. Dare to change your routine, your schedule, your habits in reading, dare to grow in your faith, dare to explore with each other in all of these areas and especially in the area of sex.

There is a common misconception that after middle age there is little need or hunger for sexual happiness. Recently at a marriage conference an older couple shared that they had sex only two times a year. Was this okay? they wondered. One of the medical doctors present replied that it was not okay; in fact, there was a danger of prostate problems for the husband. This reminded me of an elderly gentleman, a widower in his eighties, who married a seventy-five-year-old woman who had never married. When they returned from their honeymoon trip they were both aglow over their new life together. The new groom privately told my husband, "I never realized I could have so much fun at sex at the age of eighty!"

In the right setting with the right person in the right emotional climate, sex becomes a beautiful expression of love at its most divine level of happiness; that's marriage in its most enjoyable state, and I'm one of the lucky individuals who is experiencing it.

One morning as I dressed I listened to a TV talk show and heard a portion of an interview with a psychiatrist. One sentence leaped out at me: "Sexual happiness is creative energy!" I had never heard it expressed publicly before, but I have long felt that the sexual experience can release creative ideas. Therefore, my husband and I calendar mini-honeymoons no less than once a year—if possible a weekend together about four times a year. What creative solutions to problems and new ideas for work all happen in a setting of love with all other interruptions put aside!

My husband is often much more loving *away* from the bedroom and therefore I program on his calendar our "rest, retreat, restore" holiday as much as a year in advance. Husbands have a way of "burning out," so, often, after six to eight weeks of in-depth work pressure, I take Bob away to a quiet retreat where we can be very much alone and away from the pressure-producing environment. I have found I have a new man very much in love with his wife, with life, and with work, and he then does his best creative work.

A pastor in northern Scotland shared how his flock—after being snowbound in their homes for sometimes a week at a time—emerge more loving and joyous with each other, and naturally an autumn crop of babies seems to follow.

Have you ever asked why some husbands seek "mistresses" or "hookers" at out-of-town conventions? Could it be that the home, the wife, the bedroom, have become too stale? Too much the same routine? Could it be that often it is not the wife that the husband is tired of, but it is more the setting, the same nightgown, the same room? Is it possible that the wife represents responsibility and *that* spells pressure and work?

Sometimes attending a conference or seminar that is focused on marriage proves beneficial. We have participated in several and have always learned a little more about each other. It is always a great relief to find out that our marriage "problems" are really quite normal and easily solved when we hear that others have solved the same before us. One of the best-known organizations is the Marriage Encounter Movement, which is a celebration of marriage, not a clinic for troubled marriages. In response to numerous requests my husband and I have launched a Celebration of Marriage Conference, which is held annually. It is such a joy to see the many couples leave, hand in hand, with new goals for their marriage.

A successful marriage is a sex-cessful marriage, and so let me summarize twenty guidelines Bob and I have learned with and from each other through our exciting years together.

1. You will never forget the first time you have sex; therefore, save it for each other, as your first marriage experience together.
2. Married persons enjoy sex more, because sex is more than merely physical satisfaction.
3. Exciting pleasures erupt with greater passion when released from the restraints of negative subconscious emotions such as fear and guilt over exposure.
4. Eternal secrets shared in confidence and security release deeper joys!
5. Sex becomes more fun (with skilled experience with each other) as the years pass.
6. Sex begins in the mind; therefore, stimulation is vital to sexual arousal.
7. Know what turns your marriage partner *on!*
8. Know what turns your marriage partner *off!*
9. Always keep yourself attractive for each other.
10. Cleanliness is next to godliness in the sexual experience. (Your fragrance/odor can start or stop his/her motor.)
11. Dress or undress to turn each other on!
12. Variety of setting heightens sexual arousal.
13. Freedom from anticipated, unwelcomed interruptions makes a difference!
14. Compliment your lover *always!*
15. Remind your husband/wife that he/she is your only intimate relationship!

16. Respect each other *always!*
17. Never discuss your sexual experiences with others.
18. Don't take sex too seriously; relax, enjoy, and laugh with each other.
19. The greatest personal pleasure is giving your marriage partner great joy.
20. A spiritual climate will put a halo around the sexual climax; it is the icing on the cake.

It was not a surprise to us when *Redbook*'s sexual survey showed that religious couples enjoyed a greater sexual happiness than those who had no particular faith or religion. This was not only obvious in our own marriage, but it was also easy to detect in the circles of positive religious friends we have come in contact with through the years.

Among them was a beautiful retired couple in their late sixties. It was a joy to be with them, for they always treated each other with such warmth, respect, and joy. One day, this gracious lady asked if she could meet me alone sometime. Meeting me in my office a few days later, this lovely "queen" a little shyly, but with intensity, tried to impress upon me that I must write a book on "holy" sex in marriage.

I was still a young wife, married only a short time, but she shared how she and her husband have been so very happy with each other sexually. Then with tears in her eyes she shared how she and her husband often repeat the Lord's Prayer together as they lay in each other's arms after their climax.

There is a spiritual dimension to the sexual union reserved for those who truly elevate the sexual experience above the demands of much of society's understanding. It is our hope that all marriages could be blessed in heaven as ours is.

6

WORKING AS A TEAM

I am one of the lucky women who are teamed up with their husbands in career and in the management of their families. During the last few years, I've watched many wives go to work or launch a career completely independently of their husbands. I notice many marriages that remain successful and happy, but many more couples are pulled apart by their separate careers. Their "oneness" disintegrates, as their goals and life-styles lead them in opposite directions. Sometime later, when they sense they have walked to opposite poles of their lives, they feel there is little hope for happiness without dissolving their marriage relationship.

TOGETHER—IN BUSINESS

But an extra in-depth dimension appears when husbands and wives team up in their business, profession, and career. Some couples have become a team out of necessity. Vern and LaVon Dragt, successful business partners, started out in what may look like an impossible situation. Vern, a wall plasterer, was struck down with bulbar polio and confined for months to an iron lung. LaVon, desperately trying to make ends meet, left a six-week-old baby and two small girls in the care of her sister and went to work in a factory. At the end of the day, she would trade children with her sister while she went to work. Eager to find work that would not only feed the family but also allow her to spend more time with her husband and girls, LaVon took the plunge. She began selling Tupperware, a home product. Not only did she keep food on the table, but LaVon found that sales was her natural hidden talent. When Vern recovered limited use of his arms, he knew he had to learn a new trade. He went to business school and became the business manager for LaVon's fast-growing sales. Together this dynamic husband-and-wife team built one of the most successful businesses in Southern California. Their team career was born out of necessity, but disaster need not hit your family for you to consider the possibility of pooling your talents and resources.

Many of the skilled business people we depend on have team business careers. Our plumber, our cabinetmaker, and even one of our doctors all have their wives as their business managers, in charge of finances and the office.

Norma Zimmer, one of our beautiful friends, has had an outstanding career as a soloist not only for "The Lawrence Welk Show" but also on the road. Her husband is her agent and business manager. He is always at her side, coaching and giving his support. Being in their company and feeling their "at-oneness" with each other is a joy.

Not far from our home is the art studio of another successful "team career" couple. Both are gifted artists. She is the portrait artist, while her husband is known throughout the Southland for his landscapes in oil. It is an inspiring experience to enter their studio and see their enthusiasm over each other's paintings.

In 1931, a young, struggling author, Irving Stone, hired an attractive eighteen-year-old secretary to type and edit a manuscript that had been rejected seventeen times. The next publisher bought it and four days after it was released, it became a best seller. Irving married this secretary-editor. Now fifty years later they are still producing best-selling novels together. A winning team in career and marriage.

People often comment to Bob and me about our "super" marriage, but I can't disclaim the oneness we feel because we have the extra dimension of sharing our work. Our career goals have melted together. We have so much to talk about that we seldom are bored with each other. Gone is the feeling that we are living on separate and strange stages. Neither he nor I brood and wonder about the secret details of the other's eight-to-five world. We know and share the same struggles, fears, and triumphs. We know the same people. Gone is the feeling of competition. We both strive to succeed in our careers, for if one of us succeeds, we both do.

Between us flows a tremendous energy of creative ideas. As a woman, I view situations and problems differently from the way Bob does. *"Together we make a great team"* is our career slogan.

There are many unusual teams that are making a positive mark on our world, but few match the creative influence of the Buchardts, from Victoria, Canada.

Mr. Buchardt, a miner in limestone, was the most successful in his business, but his work left a giant limestone pit that gaped ugly and wide—until Mrs. Buchardt decided to turn the ugly scar of the empty mine into a place of beauty. She planned and she planted—trees, flowers, and gardens of roses. Sometimes sitting in a kitchen chair at the end of strong ropes lowered over a steep precipice, she would plant a honeysuckle vine or a climbing rose between the rocks. She then added fountains that bubbled clear fresh water. Today tourists come from around the world to see the Buchardt Gardens, alive with color and beauty. Her husband made a useful product available to the world and she teamed up with him to give us a garden of unmatched beauty.

In 1941, Jim Miller was teaching at the University of Wisconsin when he fell in love with his brightest graduate student. The following year he married her. For thirty-five years plus this husband and wife have teamed up their brilliance and scientific expertise in the laboratory and have made some exciting breakthroughs in the fight against cancer.

"The Millers, parents of two daughters, now grown, lead an

almost symbiotic life together working at desks facing each
other, commuting together," says the April 15, 1977, issue of
People magazine. They also enjoy hiking, camping, and reading together. The reporter from *People* magazine commented
that the Millers were so extraordinarily compatible that they
often finished each other's sentences. When we think "team,"
exciting things happen. Two minds *are* better than one. Great
accomplishments *are* completed by teams.

I first learned of team marriages as I watched my mother
team up with Dad in the struggle to succeed on the farm in
northwest Iowa. Year after year, season after season, crisis
after crisis, they pulled together to make ends meet from the
harvest of the crops. Together they milked the cows; together
they planted the fields; together they struggled through freez-
ing blizzards to keep their livestock alive; together they saved
their pennies to buy the farm, to send the seven children to
school.

Isn't that what marriage is really all about? Would our
brave and daring pioneers ever have survived if husbands and
wives would not have teamed up together? It is essential that
husbands think of wives as an important part of their team,
and that wives draw husbands into their careers. And it is
amazing how this team spirit strengthens the chances for
more successful careers for each of them.

What "team career" marriages do you know in your community? Have you ever considered the possibility of teaming
up with your partner in a career? What talents do you have
that complement those of your mate? What interests do you
have in common? What hobbies or special knowledge do you
have that might be the seed of a lucrative business venture?

TOGETHER—IN FAMILY MANAGEMENT

Even if your mind is blank in regard to answering these
questions, you may already be half of a winning team that
continues to be an inspiration and the backbone of our Ameri-

can society, the team of breadwinner and homemaker. When both husband and wife view the homemaker career as a most important business in our society, the team spirit thrives.

I sense a real put-down attitude toward someone who is defined as "just a homemaker." In my estimation this negative put-down is a gross misunderstanding of the expertise needed in the organization called "family" and "home."

In the past ten years, I have attended a number of conferences and seminars on executive and business management. I have also sat for long hours listening to experts in the field of top-level management. Time after time I have noted that the different categories they enumerate coincide perfectly with the problem areas of home management: budgets, personnel, motivation, and productivity. By the time our children reach adolescence, homemakers have dealt with and, it is hoped, found workable solutions for all these problems. (Not a few executives, even in government, struggle with balancing budgets.)

I contend that the management of the home is not an easy task, but when homemakers see themselves as half of a team, as "home executives"—planning budgets, solving personnel problems, and keeping the machinery running smoothly—they can be proud of their contribution to the organization.

I hear and sympathize with women's complaints of the "boredom blues." I become terribly bored with doing the same jobs, day after day. But I've also seen business executives and secretaries, even doctors and nurses, who get sick of their daily routines. Seeing their locked-in schedules make me thankful for the great freedom that, as a homemaker, I have to change my routine from one day to the next.

Perhaps it would be most helpful for young parents to attend a management or business seminar together with the idea of applying these techniques and principles to their families and homes. In every management course I took we were taught to manage by objectives, which is to say we should:

1. Clarify our values.
2. Establish priorities.
3. Set goals.
4. Make decisions.
5. Calculate the resources needed to reach the goals and carry out the decisions.
6. Review and adjust our resources (time, money, energy) to accommodate our carefully selected objectives.
7. Establish a calendar, setting time limits on decisions to make sure we don't procrastinate.
8. Set aside "meeting times" where "the team" reviews progress made toward realizing our determined objectives.

In summary, we are shaping our future by making decisions, i.e., committing ourselves to carrying out manageable and measurable objectives that—in essence is what I mean by M.B.O.—management by objectives. The alternative? To set no goals and simply drift along, allowing other pressures and people to pull our lives apart and push our lives around.

I found that I had to, and could, manage a marriage, a home, and a family by objectives. If more "family executives" would apply the M.B.O. principles, there would be an exciting resurrection of positive attitudes toward the team business we call "the home"!

Why not sit down with your spouse and together establish your family objectives? Will you work toward "becoming one" in every sense? Exactly how and where could you start fusing your separate interests into one? Go ahead, think big! Brainstorm and write down possibilities that may, now, seem utterly impossible. Dream of the togetherness that could become a part of your everyday lives—whether it is in actually sharing a business career or in sharing the joy of family management.

7

COPING WITH CLUTTER, CLATTER, KIDS, AND CASH

Why is it that babies always come when we really can't afford them? I've often imagined how easy life might have been if I could have faced the birth of our babies with cash in the bank—enough to pay for the hospital bills, the doctor, the extra diapers, the extra help I could have used at home.

Is there any way to adequately prepare for having a family? Even today, with birth control and baby-preparation classes, I still see apprehension in the eyes of young couples. How well my husband and I know the feeling!

With every pregnancy, the same questions haunted me: How was this new baby going to change my life-style? Would I really be able to handle the change? Do I really have the wherewithal to be a wise and capable parent?

When we married, there was no birth control except the rhythm method, which worked for us only one month. We had no hospital insurance, owned no baby furniture, attended no how-to classes. We were two very unprepared people who had intended to wait two years so we could adequately care for our first baby.

We were married one month after Bob graduated from

seminary. After a weekend honeymoon near our home in
Iowa, we moved to a suburb of Chicago to our first parish.

Away from our parents and close relatives, we had to rely
on "new" friends, all of them acquaintances of ten months or
less. With a baby shower (which saved the day) and a bor-
rowed baby bed, we became the scared parents of our very
own first baby.

If I was scared, my husband was terrified. I had learned a
few essentials from babysitting jobs through my school years.
Also, I had younger brothers and sisters and knew a little
about the responsibility that comes with little ones. However,
Bob was the youngest, by many years, in his family. In fact,
he was a change-of-life baby, an "accident." We have often
asked the question, "What if abortion had been as widely
practiced then as it is now?"

Leaving home for college at the age of sixteen, Bob had
spent seven years in the academic world. He lived in dormi-
tories, far away from children, especially babies. He was completely baffled by fatherhood. If there were books that could
have prepared us, we couldn't afford to buy them, so, suddenly, here we were, responsible for a squirming bundle that
was always either wet or hungry. Many days I wanted to go
home and cry on my mother's shoulder and say, "What do I
do now?" but fortunately she was too far away, so Bob and I
had to deal with each crisis. That in itself drew us together in
such a way that, even today, we are blessed with an extra
reliance on each other.

We brought Sheila, our firstborn, home on a cold, rainy
morning in April. Bob tried so hard to heat the house, but the
coal furnace would not fire fast enough. He tried to sweep the
house clean, but in the process raised so much dust that two
weeks later he came home with a vacuum cleaner. (It took us
over a year to pay for it!)

That evening he tried to fix dinner, another first for him. He
mixed a can of beans with raw hamburger, but the beans
burned before the hamburger was cooked. Muttering under

his breath, I heard a new sentence that he would repeat often over the next years. "This is enough to make a preacher cuss!"

Just then the doorbell rang. Two of our denominational representatives had stopped in for dinner and overnight lodging. (This was not an unusual request made of pastors who lived along the main highway south of Chicago.)

Whether they caught the not too appealing fragrance from the kitchen, or whether it was Sheila's wailing cry, or the bewildered look on our faces, I don't know, but they said farewell in less than one half hour, a most unusual occurrence! And so began our introduction to glorious parenthood.

Three and one half years later, little Bob joined our family. Followed, three years later, by Jeanne. Seven years later Carol was born and two years later Gretchen arrived.

Would we change any of it, now that we look back to the skinned knees, the sleepless nights, the tired days, the crabby babies? We experienced all that comes with parenthood, but we would not change the ages, the sex, the numbers, the names, the appearances, the characteristics of any of our children. Each one is so super; Bob and I are rich indeed as we enjoy the wealth of our family relationships.

I can't help but feel that the Almighty has a way of preparing parents throughout the nine months of waiting. During one of my first pregnancies, I came across a prayer of an expectant mother that went something like this:

"Dear God, there is within me a living human being created in Your image. I sense I am on the brink of being a part of Your miracle of creation. Thank you for Your trust in me. Give me the wisdom to so live that this tiny life that stirs within me now, may know You as I know You, my Friend, my Counselor, my Savior. Amen."

Surely, of all the negative decisions that are made today, there is none more negative than that of *abortion*. I remember a very troubled and ailing old woman, perhaps in her late seventies, who came to my husband and me after a worship service. Trembling, she asked to see us privately. Breaking down in sobs, she confessed that over forty years before she had aborted a baby girl. Throughout her entire life she had been haunted by this act. If the baby had lived what would she be like today? She had often imagined what she would have named this girl. She pictured at various ages this daughter she had never allowed to live. Assuring her of God's forgiveness, we comforted her as best as we could, but both Bob and I have always remembered the sorrow that this woman carried as a result of choosing a negative solution to her problem!

It takes adjustment to suddenly have a twenty-four-hour, 365-days-a-year, eighteen-year-long responsibility put on your shoulders, but I was amazed at how quickly Bob and I adapted. And now we watch our married children adjusting in much the same way. We thought nothing of packing up our baby to take her shopping, to church, on a trip. Where we went, she went.

PRACTICAL PARENTING

What are some of the practical do's that we learned from wiser and older parents? The first two of these especially apply to mothers.

1. *Don't forget Daddy!* Because of a mother's physical nine-month-long attachment to her baby, it is easy for her to get her priorities backward. That six-foot guy at her side still comes before the helpless infant in her arms. A new baby automatically demands first "dibs" on a mother's time and attention, but Daddy needs to know that he is not going to be forgotten or have to take the backseat from here on in. So, date night is *even more* important.

2. *Mothers need a "be-nice-to-me" day once a month (at least).* Because of our weekly date night, one day a month away from the house was enough for me. How I looked forward to "Mother's day out." I saved my pennies to afford

lunch at a lovely downtown restaurant with another friend who shared the same tastes in music, food, and leisure that I do. We talked endlessly, first about our families. We laughed a lot, enjoyed special "girl" talk, exchanging latest tips on cosmetics or clothes. We sometimes cried together, sharing a hurt. We would get into each other's world, but mostly we needed to get away from our own responsibilities for a few hours, and that has been and continues to be a healing therapy. How inviting the family and house seem the next day. Just getting away from all the interruptions for a while returned my healthy outlook on life.

I believe the most difficult adjustment of having children was that I seldom, if ever, finished a project without first having laid it aside to change a diaper, and later to fix a peanut butter sandwich or wipe a drippy nose. As the family grew up, the interruptions changed in description, but there are still multitudes of them. Long ago I learned to take a positive attitude toward interruptions and tell myself daily: "I wonder how boring life would be without all these interruptions?"

3. *A good reliable babysitter* is a most important investment. We were not afraid to pay a little more money, if it assured us of good care. Since our parents lived in other states we never had the luxury of having Grandma as a babysitter we could call at any time. Therefore, we adopted a "Grandma" or "Aunt" for each of our children. The children accepted these "God-sent angels," known as our "California Grandmas," as their own. In fact, if time passed by without seeing them for a while, they would ask, "When is Grandma coming?"

But I soon made an interesting observation. By the time I had used up my babysitting budget for the month, the children were restless and frustrated. They needed the security of Dad and Mom being home. So the dollar shortage that forced us to stay home was a blessing for all of us.

Then, we still "trade" children with other families today. Our teens will visit at their friends' home while we are gone

on an overnight trip, and our teens' friends come to visit us
when their families are gone for a weekend. This makes a
"parents' holiday," a treat for the children as well.

4. *Enjoy each stage and each age!* How easily this is said,
and how difficult to do. But believe it or not, children do
grow up rapidly.

Arthur Gordon, in *A Touch of Wonder*,* tells how one day,
when he was thirteen and his brother ten, his father promised
to take them to the circus. But at lunchtime, an urgent phone
call came requiring their father's attention to his business.
Arthur, bracing himself for a great disappointment, was
greatly relieved to hear his father say, "No, I can't come. It
will have to wait!"

When his father joined the family again, his mother added
her words: "The circus keeps coming back, you know!"

The wise father answered, "I know, but childhood doesn't!"

5. *Learn to laugh at yourself and teach your children to
laugh*—not only in response to a TV program, but as the result of a fun time with you. How often Erma Bombeck has
brightened my day, filling my heart with good medicine.
Laughter is a divine release mechanism built in each of us to
relieve tension and stress. What a healthy emotional exercise
for all of us.

April Fools' Day has always been a fun day at our house.
Usually the children would put salt in the sugar bowl, sugar
in the saltshaker, and enjoy their daddy's reaction when, un-
suspecting, he would take his first bite of cereal sprinkled
with salt. One April Fools' Day, Bob felt it was his turn to
pull a joke on the children. Before we awakened them, Bob
put all the clocks ahead one hour. Then he ran to the children's bedrooms and called, "Hurry, hurry, we overslept! You
will be late for school!" How the children jumped and ran to
look first at one clock, then the other. Then they dashed
about, dressing frantically to get to school on time. When
they were almost dressed, their father shouted, "April fool!"
The children, shocked, ran to the telephone to ask for time,

* Fleming Revell, 1974.

and, yes, it was true! It truly was an April Fools' joke. What laughter and squeals took place for the next fifteen minutes as the children chased their dad through the house.

6. *Since there is no such person as "the perfect parent," become a realistic, happy "imperfect parent."* It was the day after Christmas and the family was all excited, for we were taking a train from California to Iowa for my husband's parents' fiftieth wedding anniversary. But there was something wrong with both Sheila and Bobby. They weren't feeling up to par and both had some sores—Sheila under her arm and Bobby around his mouth. Just to make sure, I had taken them to the doctor, and he had diagnosed them both as having impetigo. Both received a penicillin shot and some ointment, and we were on our way.

On the second day of the train ride, one mother questioned me about the sore on Bobby's face and with a confident voice of authority, I assured her it was impetigo, well under control with medication.

Upon our arrival in Iowa, both children broke out with severe cases of chicken pox. There were chicken pox on their faces, in their throats, in their ears, on the bottom of their feet —everywhere! I felt so badly that we had exposed to the disease all those families and children on the train. But I had to realize that I had acted in good faith. I had taken them to a doctor. I had followed his advice. I was not guilty of being irresponsible nor had I intentionally exposed those families. I had done what any good mother would have done, and I had to forgive myself for having insufficient knowledge.

That was only one of our imperfect acts as parents.

Another very serious mistake I made as a parent was to leave six-month-old Carol with my sister, Winnie, for eight weeks as I joined my husband for a long-dreamed-of pilgrimage to the Holy Land. The children were tremendously excited about visiting the farm in Iowa, but I was nervous about leaving them for so long. However, I felt that Carol would be too young to miss us, and besides, Winnie was ecstatic about having a baby in the house. She had always

wanted a large family and many babies, although that had
not been God's plan for her. She had nearly lost her life in
childbirth with her second child ten years before.

I rested in the knowledge that Carol would have better
care and attention than I could give her, but I was not
prepared for her rejection of me upon our return. Not only
did she not know Bob and me, she wanted nothing to do with
us. She screamed when I went near her. Later a psychologist
friend of ours explained that six to eight months after birth is
the most insecure time in a young child's life. When we left,
she never knew the difference between my sister and me, but
a month later, my voice and touch were foreign to her.

How we managed through the first days and weeks after
our return, I do not remember. From August to December,
Carol awoke every night, and stood in her crib. She cried and
cried and cried. When Bob or I would take turns picking her
up, trying to console her, she wanted nothing to do with us.
We were both tremendously concerned that we had perma-
nently damaged her emotional stability, but we continued to
believe that love would prevail. At last, Carol slept through
one night, then two, and she became again the happy, con-
tented child she had been before we left.

Thirteen years later, when Carol was visiting relatives again
in Iowa, I stepped into the intensive care room where Carol
was lying still and swollen, under oxygen, with tubes protruding from many areas of her broken body. There was my sister,
again giving her love and support to our Carol. Somehow, I
felt that God knew our fun-loving, adventurous Carol would
then need more than one set of parents as her support system.
I saw the providence of God had worked through my imper-
fection to the benefit of us all. We "see through a glass
darkly" and have no idea how today's "mistakes" may prove
to be tomorrow's blessings!

The second part of our rule for imperfect parents is just as
important as the first. *Let the children know you are not perfect!*

We do a terrible injustice to our children if we give them

the image that we are perfect, we know all the answers. There is already a natural belief as a child grows up that God, Mom, and Dad are perfect, and that "I have to be good, do good, so they will continue to love me." The fear of failure overwhelms adults and children alike, causing emotional and physical breakdowns. Therefore we need to admit to our children and young people that we are not all-knowing. Of course, we must have firm principles or rules. We must have enough confidence in ourselves and in our decisions to stand firm and not be wishy-washy and namby-pamby.

When our children challenge our decisions, we often say, "This is our decision and we made it with all the knowledge that was available to us at the time. Someday, when you are a parent, you will need to make decisions as best as you can. Then you will better understand how difficult it is to know what choice will prove to be the best."

7. *Dare to have distinctive rules!* Each of our children learned that because we are "Schullers" we have distinct rules in our home. For instance, we have never given the children automatic allowances. Because my husband and I both grew up in a farming community in Iowa, we were conditioned in the "no-work, no-eat" philosophy which we both feel is a healthy, highly motivating attitude. Even though there is a great movement away from this philosophy, it still is common sense to teach our children that you need to "give in order to receive." For if all of us adopted the let-someone-else-do-the-work attitude, there would be no food to eat.

Because we provide each of our children with a warm bed, good food, and clothes to wear, they, in turn, must help with the family "maintenance." The least they can do is to make their bed, pick up their clothes, take turns helping with the daily chores. For completing these tasks, they receive no allowance. If there are special jobs, such as washing the family car, cleaning the garage, doing extra dishes, or acting as waiter or waitress when we entertain large groups, then they may earn spending money.

An extra bonus to this rule is that it teaches our children

that work can be enjoyable. What a blessing for them, for the
alternative is to lead them into a life of boredom and illness.
Recently a friend who has been seriously ill for over two
years told us that she was going back to work part time because she was sure that not having anything to do was ham-
pering her complete recovery. This wise woman went on to
explain that she was depressed as a result of boredom, and as
she described her upcoming work projects, there was a
healthier enthusiasm and new hope in her voice.

Another distinctive rule in our home is: When other children come over to play, it is up to our youngsters to inform
their friends of our rules.

One day when Carol was only nine, I overheard one of her
friends use language that is not permitted in our home. Every
other sentence seemed to be accented with crude words that
we called "barnyard language." They were not allowed in our
farm homes where Bob and I grew up, even though it was not
uncommon for other farm workers to use this kind of language in the barnyard.

I waited for Carol's response, before I attempted to take
the situation under control. Finally, Carol spoke up. "Joey, we
don't use those words in our house. If you want to play here,
you had better use nice words or Mom will wash out your
mouth, and that tastes terrible." She then went into a vivid
description of the awful-tasting soap we used. "It smells all
right, but the taste is the awfulest you can imagine." Little
Joey tried hard to watch her language, but she became a less
frequent visitor during the coming weeks.

Of course, it is tempting for us to give in when our children
complain, "Everyone else is doing it. Why can't we?" But the
easiest response isn't always the best. Children need the security of knowing that rules are firm and distinctively *ours*.

8. *Dare to discipline!* Isn't it wonderful how the Almighty
planned the human anatomy so that we can dare to discipline
without harming our children.

Spanking our small children's bare bottoms with bare hands
reaffirmed who was boss and restored law and order. Later

the bare-bottom spankings were replaced with the capturing of car keys or other dramatic demonstrations of discipline.

I shall never forget one day—and I daresay she will not either—when Carol was only two years and three months old. We had just brought our new Gretchen home from the hospital. One morning after Carol had dressed and eaten her breakfast, I put her into the backyard to play with our collie puppy. Checking to make sure she was safe inside the fenced yard with the gate firmly closed, I proceeded to bathe, dress, and feed our new baby.

Some time later, I went to check on Carol, but neither she nor the puppy was in sight. I quickly put the baby down and ran outside to look around the corner. In dismay, I saw that the back gate was wide open. I ran to the street and looked both ways. I ran back into the garage, then the alley, but there was no sight of Carol. I called her loudly, but the only response was the pounding of my heart. I went to the telephone to call some of our neighbors. Few answered their phones and those who did answer said, "No, I have not seen Carol."

By now, I was frantic. How did she get the gate open? When had she learned how? After checking the backyard and the garage again, I started down the street. As I approached the corner, I looked far ahead of me, and there almost a block away, was a uniformed policeman holding the hand of a tiny girl, and carrying a puppy in his arms.

"Does she belong to you? She's much too small to be playing alone in the park near the creek. She's lucky she wasn't hit by a car or drowned!" With an admonishing tone of voice, he scolded Carol, but he was really scolding me. I was too shaken to reply. I knew why Carol had found the park. That was an after-school treat for her, when either Jeanne, Bob, or Sheila took her to the park for an outing.

When we arrived home, Gretchen was crying, but I first took Carol, and, shaking her oh, so hard, I said, "Don't you ever go out the back gate again." I spanked her bottom and shook her again. Now all three of us were crying—Gretchen,

Carol, and Mom. Carol never again went near the gate. She knew the result would not be a happy one.

Recently, a remarkably successful parent said to us, "We never said no to our children."

In amazement, my husband and I both looked at her and said, "How could you *not* say no?" Her reply was most interesting.

"It's very simple," she said. "Our answer is either 'Yes, if' or 'Yes, when' or 'Yes, but.'

"'May I watch television?'

"'Yes, when your homework is finished!' or 'Yes, if it is one of our approved programs.'" So, she said, if your daughter asks if she can sleep with her boyfriend, you don't say no, you simply say, "Yes, when you marry him!"

This was an unusual approach to discipline and I daresay a most positive approach, although I'm not sure it would work for us.

In our home we try not to say a dogmatic no without giving a good reason why, and we always try to propose an alternative action. When our children want to go to a party that we sense is not well chaperoned or the wrong kind of party, we suggest that a friend join him or her for a night at Disneyland, or we give some other special-treat night as an alternative. We find very little resentment or rebellion when (1) we give a good reason why we say no and (2) we give an alternative event as a choice.

It is of the utmost importance to be united as parents in the area of discipline. How often our children will ask each of us the same question at different times, hoping that one of us will agree to their request. More than once, I have heard the children say, "Daddy says we can . . . ," or to Bob, they will say, "Mommy says we can. . . ."

Our reply is a consistent one: "Well, if Daddy says you can, then I shall discuss it with him," and vice versa. "United we stand, divided we fall" has been the success slogan that gives a stronger dimension of discipline.

When Bob is at work or out of town, and one of the chil-

dren has become involved in what I consider a serious problem, I will let them know that it is so serious that we will
have to discuss it together when Dad gets home. Oftentimes
this wait for the punishment is more effective than the punishment itself.

Our third rule for discipline is to discipline the offending
child in private and not in front of brothers, sisters, and other
people. That's only the kind thing to do. Self-esteem is fragile,
and to be corrected is in itself a wounding experience without
adding the deeper wound of embarrassment. If this rule were
practiced in school classrooms, would there be more confident
youngsters daring to reach for higher goals, because their self-
esteem would be without the scars of embarrassment?

9. *Teach the positives!* The most important ingredient we,
as parents, need to teach our children is the difference between *positive* and *negative* thinking. Allow these words to
become a part of the daily vocabulary of your home. Teach
them to believe in their ability. And that can happen only
when we, as parents, believe the best about our children. As I
read the stories of people who have made a significant influence for good in our world, without an exception, they give
credit to a parent or parents who "believed in me."

One day as we were out for a drive we passed a meadow of
grazing horses. Bobby, then age ten, spoke up from the backseat. "I'm going to get me a horse when I grow up!"

Bob and I looked at each other and again Bobby repeated
his emphatic exclamation, "I'm going to get me a horse!" Bob
questioned little Bobby, whose bright brown eyes sparkled
with joyful expectation.

"What makes you think you're going to get a horse?"

"You said so," was Bobby's reply to his father. "You said,
practice positive thinking and your dreams will come true!"

My heart sank within me. Our yard was a small city lot.
Where would we keep a horse? And how could we ever
afford one, even if we had the room?

Bob, however, replied, "O.K., Bobby, I have no doubt that
you will get your horse if you want one bad enough."

I did not have the faith to believe his wish would come true, but two years later, Bobby went to spend the summer on the Schuller farm in Iowa. There he found a horse named Sunshine, which Bob's brother, Henry, boarded for several years. Bobby felt he had his horse. He was allowed to ride, feed, and care for Sunshine as if it were his own. A few years later Bobby became interested in another kind of horse—the horsepower of a car motor—and the dream took on a new angle.

How thankful we are today that we somehow sensed the importance of stressing positive attitudes to our children. It will remain our most valuable inheritance to them.

APPRECIATE YOUR OWN GREEN GRASS

Finally, when I have difficulty coping with the house's clutter and clatter, I think of all the homes and families that don't begin to have the good life-style we enjoy. Instead of looking at the greener grass on the other side of the fence, I have developed the habit of thinking of the mothers who care for small children on the sampans in Hong Kong or in high-rise apartments above that city. What problems they must have as they live either on the houseboats on the dirty harbor, or in crowded rooms with only one bathroom for many families. Or I find myself thinking of the mothers who must work in the hot fields with their babies strapped to their backs. Or I think again of the young twelve- and thirteen-year-old mothers in New Guinea with only a thatched roof for shelter and a machete and bamboo pole for their only tools, cooking dinner in a hole in the ground, no medicine nearby, and bound by a primitive way of life. Or I think of the poverty-stricken areas of India where we wept at the sight of these villages with hordes of children playing in the dirt. No shade trees or cool green grass. Then there are the young Chinese girls I watched, in mainland China one hot summer, mixing and carrying cement. Or when I resent all the laundry or cooking, I think of the many Korean women I saw who washed their clothes in a cold mountain stream and cooked in outdoor kitchens. How rich, how fortunate, how grateful I am for my family and home.

The first Christmas we spent in Garden Grove was a meager one indeed. Our paychecks were sent to us from our headquarters in New York. But with the Christmas mail rush, we did not receive the December 15 nor December 30 check until after the new year. We had already taken a cut in our salary when we moved to California, and it was quite a feat for four of us to live on our tight budget of twenty dollars a week. When those checks did not come, day after day, we became nervous indeed. I was mixing whole milk with powdered milk to fool the children. We were buying day-old bread, to squeeze a few more days out of what money we had left.

None of us remember what we gave each other for Christmas that year, but Sheila remembers going with us to convalescent homes to sing Christmas carols and bring a little joy into the lives of older shut-ins. Even little Bob, though he was too young to sing, was a blessing to them, as they so seldom saw toddlers.

I remember making and decorating Christmas candles out of used wax stubs from the church, and these were our gifts to friends that year.

We remember joining our church groups in distributing baskets of groceries to homes that were poorer than we. Then, on Christmas morning, we opened many beautiful gifts of food from friends and neighbors, which held us over. We believed in the positive, and God was faithful. We looked for the joys of Christmas, and found them.

How can you cope with clutter, clatter, cash, and kids? I know of one sure way: keep a positive faith going and glowing. Believe in yourself; you can handle it! Pressures? Tommy LaSorda told us one day, "Pressure is only the fear of failure; I don't believe in it." Believe and you will achieve—in the success of a great family.

Believe in yourself and believe in each other. Life in a family is a rich experience when we train ourselves to look and count all the positives.

Whenever I have a difficult time coping with the clutter and clatter of the family, we join with other positive parents who affirm us and become our support system. About fifteen years ago I became concerned about the lack of support groups for young mothers. When we announced in our weekly church paper the forming of such a group, they responded enthusiastically. Through the years this support group continues to give positive encouragement and strength to many who have chosen the rich life through *positive parenthood!*

8

HOW TO LIVE WITH YOUR TEEN AND LIKE IT

One of the birthdays we celebrate with the most flourish is our children's thirteenth. Months ahead, our about-to-be teenager would remind us, "Only three more months and I'm no longer a child; I'll be a teenager, and you know what that means, don't you, Mom?" "What *does* that mean?" becomes a new and confusing issue between parent and teen. Both wanting the same goal, but each on a different end of the pendulum.

As I write this chapter on the eve of the thirteenth birthday of our last child, I remember the multitude of emotions, the countless frustrations and accomplishments we have experienced with our four teenagers.

Of all the years of childhood, I believe that the most traumatic and dramatic one is the thirteenth year. One day they want complete freedom. "Treat me as an adult," they say, but at the first sign of difficulty, or even without any warning, our new teens cry out for the cuddling and attention they received as a small child. One minute our teen girls dressed and acted like twenty-year-olds, the next minute they wanted to sit on Daddy's lap and just be cuddled.

One of the most tragic mistakes parents make is assuming that teens are adults. The parents may be so relieved that their child is now grown up that they actually encourage and sometimes push the teen to make decisions too large and responsibilities too heavy to assume without the guidance, control, and wisdom of concerned parents.

Finding a right balance between letting go of apron strings and overprotecting them is not easy, but I have watched too many parents, out of fear, not wisdom, become overly permissive and disaster for the teen has resulted.

In the late nineteen-fifties the Rev. Dr. and Mrs. Raymond Beckering were serving in a parish in a wealthy suburb of Los Angeles during the junior high years of their only daughter, Hope. We watched their wise parenting of their young teen as she faced the tremendous pressures of the school and community to be involved in partying, dating, and other social functions that were far too adult for her thirteen- and fourteen-year-old emotions. The father (Uncle Ray, as he was affectionately known by our children) spent many hours with his daughter, involving her energies and time in a hobby that demanded many disciplines: the care of dogs for showing in dog shows. How busy he kept her, dog show after dog show. Meanwhile, her mother, noticing that Hope was interested in creating fashions, enrolled her in sewing classes and worked closely with her, encouraging her to design and make doll clothes. She soon had a little business, as she created, made, and dressed dolls for sale. When we would visit, Hope would be excited about a new ribbon she had won in a dog show, and always she displayed two or three new dolls dressed in original fashions, ready to be picked up by their new owners.

Today, Hope is a successful teacher, happily married to a leading government official. A neighbor girl of Hope's age, deprived of this wise parenting, today is in our state prison serving a life sentence.

How does a parent know which choices are wise and which foolish? When should you say yes and when no? Often it is

easier to let them go their own way than it is to take the time
to direct them in a right direction. You then avoid scenes and
showdowns, but a parent needs to expect the tremendous
emotional instability that accompanies physical puberty.
Scenes and showdowns are unavoidable during this stage.

One day teens are so loving, kind, and thoughtful that we,
as parents, relax and enjoy the wonderful feeling of having at-
tained success. Then only hours later when we dare to say no,
the subsequent wrath and tantrums try our patience, and
demand much more wisdom, love, guidance, and firmness.
The scenario will repeat time and again before our precious
teen will have grown into a wise, responsible, and happy
adult.

In all areas of intimate marriage and family living, we need
to be positive . . . positive . . . positive, always affirming, but
especially during the teen years.

When Sheila, our eldest daughter, was in sixth grade, Bob
and I attended the seventh-grade orientation presented by the
principal of the junior high school that Sheila would be attending. We will eternally be grateful for his wise counsel
and advice, which we have practiced with all our teens.

MAKE SURE YOUR TEEN HAS A GOAL!

This wise educator compared in depth the difference between his junior high pupils who had no goals, and therefore
no channel for their unmeasurable energy, and those pupils
who focused on a goal, directing that same powerful energy
toward a specific purpose. It did not matter, he said, if the
teen changed his or her goal during the high school years, but
not having a goal made teens much more difficult to work and
live with.

Our sixteen years of experience in parenting teens has
proven him right. Although I am no psychologist, I see that
one of the major benefits of this goal setting is that it distracts

them from the puzzling physical changes taking place in their bodies. Their world, then, is broader than "doing your own thing," "I'm now grown up," or "sex."

Teenagers feel and act in extremes. For the most part, they know nothing of "little involvement," or the "middle of the road," or the commonsense approach to decision making. "I've fallen in love," "I hate that teacher," "I hate you," "I wish he were dead," "This meal is gross," are only some of the all-or-nothing statements that reveal the way in which a teen looks at the world in general.

So when our children reach the age of thirteen they need to know what they want to do with their God-given gift of life. Only one lifetime, what will you do? What do you like to do? What are you good at? When a teen has more than one goal, so much the better, because a variety of activities will keep his or her interest concentrated on the future.

Discipline is a by-product of commitment to a goal. I cannot say enough about the influence sports and music have had in disciplining the life-style and habits of our teens. The long hours of practice, the unending striving for perfection, taught our teens that success is really spelled W-O-R-K. Muscles soon get flabby without exercise, and fingers, without practice, stumble over the piano keys.

A physical goal develops character, but it also releases frustration. How often I have watched each of our teens, when angry at the world, go out in the backyard and angrily throw a ball against the wall over and over again, or bounce the basketball in anger until his or her arm would wearily drop to the side. They have physically released emotional energy by practicing a skill.

At the age of five each of our five children had to study piano privately. Because music was "in the genes" of my husband's family and mine, we wanted our children to have the discipline and knowledge that would enable them to enjoy music even if they did not pursue a musical career. When they became teenagers, this discipline gave them an outlet for negative and positive emotions. They expressed their joy, excitement, success, and also anger, resentment, and frustration at the piano, or on the guitar behind the closed bedroom door. Sometimes they played very loudly. Often very long. But sooner or later I could sense the calming of their spirit. The music would stop and our teen would be ready to talk or to dismiss the entire episode, having resolved it through this release of emotion.

What does a goal do for a teen? The dedication of young energy and bright wisdom gives *direction* for a fantastic future and forms *discipline* for a creative life-style free from ruinous habits.

KNOW WHERE YOUR TEEN IS AT ALL TIMES

This was the second rule the junior high principal shared that night sixteen years ago.

How shocked and disappointed I was. I expected to relax with our eldest daughter, now that she was in junior high. I soon learned that our teen needed more careful observation and concentration than the preschooler in our home. At seven-thirty or eight at night I could tuck our preschooler in bed and for the most part be free of constant care until morning. But over the years, I've lost more sleep waiting up for a teen than I have tending sick babies.

Some time ago when our entire family, married children, college age—young and old—gathered around our dinner table, Jeannie, then a junior in high school, asked if she could go out with some friends the following evening. Before my husband or I could ask the usual questions, our married son, Bob, replied and rattled off with concise rapidity the five questions he knew he was about to hear.

1. What are you going to do?
2. Where are you going to be?
3. Who are you going to be with?
4. What time are you leaving and returning?
5. Who is driving?

Recently a mother told me, "My parents' rule was that we had to be in at midnight, but now that I'm a mother of a teen, that is too vague for me. If Lori is going to an early movie, especially with a date, and the movie is going to finish at ten, then I need to know their plans between ten and twelve or she will find herself saying good night at ten-thirty."

We have never allowed our teens to go out for a day or a night with friends or dates unless they could tell us their specific agenda. If their answers to the five crucial questions were vague, they stayed home or friends were invited over to our house. If the answer was bowling, they had better be bowling. If the answer was the movies, which movie at which theater?

Know where your teen is at all times. Wow! What a responsibility, but what a relief to know where they are.

One night our son, Bob, a senior in high school, was scheduled for babysitting at home. When my husband and I returned at 9:30 P.M., Bob was not there. The children said he had gone over to Cecil's house. Upset that he would leave the younger children, I called Cecil's home, only to hear, "No, Bob is not here, and I haven't seen him tonight."

An hour later Bob walked through the doorway to face two angry parents. "Where have you been, Bob? Don't you realize that you walked out on a big responsibility?"

We looked him directly in the eye. "I've been to Cecil's; I had a problem with homework," was his verbal reply.

"We telephoned Cecil's house, and Cecil said you have not been there tonight. Where were you?"

With guilt all over his face, Bob looked at us and in a tiny voice for his six-foot-three, 170-pound frame, he said, "I was at Linda's house."

Bob long remembered that night. His punishment? Bob's father, who had been drinking coffee from one of my many cherished teacups, dramatically threw the empty cup onto the hard floor, breaking it into many pieces. "There, Bob, that's what has happened to our trust in you. You have shattered it! How can we trust you again? Trust is a most beautiful thing

—more beautiful than this teacup. You are grounded until you have this cup all put together again—each little piece. When the cup is whole again, we will talk."

It took some weeks for Bob painstakingly to glue each small piece in place, and when it was finished, he found that tiny slivers here and there were lost for good. The mended cup sat on Bob's dresser for the remaining years through high school and college. The last I saw of it was when he packed his keepsakes up to move into his first new home with his bride, *Linda*.

PEERS' AND PARENTS' PRESSURE

In the summer of 1976 my husband and I attended the International Psychological Congress, held for five days in Paris, France. Participants came from the United States, from all of Europe, and from behind the Iron Curtain. Through instant translation the congress benefited professors and students from many different cultures. While my husband attended in-depth studies on topics such as behavior modification and group psychology, I attended seminars dealing with children, teens, and family. One entire morning we focused on the influence of peer pressure. The various lectures and papers presented that day reaffirmed some of the conclusions I had already drawn from firsthand experiences.

The influence of peer pressure is a powerful yet normal part of life for the teenager and for adults. One of my husband's often-quoted sayings is:

WE HEAR THROUGH OUR PEERS AND NOT OUR EARS.

As teens become more and more impressed with the actions and reactions of their peers, they are less concerned about what their parents think or expect of them.

When we parents sense our teens withdrawing from us or disagreeing or arguing with us, we must be sure we react

with pure motives. Are we upset because the child is bringing
harm to him or herself? Are we threatened that our child is
growing up and we are losing our control? Are we suffering
from battered egos?

One morning our doorbell rang, and I was surprised to see
an acquaintance at my door. She seemed troubled and asked
if she could talk. A little older than I, she always impressed
me with her charming personality and attractive appearance.
This particular morning she wore no makeup, and, in tears,
she shared that her college daughter was receiving poor
grades, and besides that, she was now sleeping with her boyfriend.

More distressing to me than this news, however, was the
mother's reaction to the problem. She went on to say that her
family was her pride and joy, her life. How could her daughter do this to her—the model mother of the ideal family?
How could she face her neighbors, her church friends? This
mother's sorrow was not for her daughter's future but for her
own deflated ego, *her* image.

We, as parents, must equip our teens to become adults. We
must not view them as extensions of ourselves, but as people
in their own right who must someday carry their own responsibilities.

How do we cope with this growing up and growing away
attitude?

1. Before your child becomes a teen, make sure your neigh-
borhood, church, or social circle will provide potential positive peers for your impressionable children.

2. Know who your teen's peers are. This will explain your
teen's new habits or attitudes. A survey conducted in Canada,
the results of which we saw at our study in Paris, shows that
most frequently a teen's peers are of the opposite sex and
slightly older, usually school friends. Older cousins also rated
high on the list. Teachers and clergy rated lowest.

3. Don't fear their growing up or, when it happens, feel
that you are failing as a parent. This negative reaction will
only produce a negative response. Remain firm on the princi-

ples you have set forth as a family, yet continue to love and affirm your teen.

When Sheila was in junior high she became acquainted with two friends who were twin sisters a little older than herself. They all walked home from school together. Soon the twins were spending more and more time at our house. I was troubled when I overheard them constantly putting down their parents. They came out with daily extreme statements such as "I could kill my father!" "I hate my mother." The conversation I would overhear coming from these two girls was so distressing that I talked with Sheila, trying to understand why they were so negative and resentful. I closed the conversation agreeing with Sheila that I would not forbid her to associate with the twins, unless I saw a change in Sheila's attitude toward us. I hopefully suggested to her that, even though she was outnumbered, she might influence them to become more positive.

Some weeks passed and the twins continued their constant negative barrage on their parents. I noticed Sheila's attitude growing more impatient and sharp with me and the rest of the family. Again I warned her of our agreement concerning the twins. One day, an "I hate you!" came from the lips of our loving Sheila, in response to a chore I had asked her to complete. That was it! Her relationship with the twins would have to end. That was easier to decide than to solve the "How to do it?" What would Sheila tell them? With whom would she now walk home? How could she avoid them?

I decided that Sheila would be too busy to have time for the twins. If they came to the door or if they telephoned, Sheila would be busy practicing piano, or helping me. As for the walking home from school, I had to do some fast thinking. The first day, I picked up Sheila at school and took her shopping for a new pair of shoes we had delayed in buying. I shifted my entire schedule around so we always had some errand to run after school. Piano lessons were rescheduled from Saturday to weekday afternoons. I urged Sheila to try out for after-school plays and music rehearsals. It was oftentimes inconvenient to drop a special project and pack up the baby to chauffeur Sheila from school, but it was one of the most intelligent decisions I made as a parent.

Sheila's "busyness" soon became a bore for the twins. They found new friends to walk home with and Sheila found more *positive* peers through her new "positive busyness" in music and art.

Judge Price Daniels from Texas met our teen and college-aged young people at a reception some time ago, and, apparently impressed with our three positive teens, asked us the question, "How do you keep your teens from rebelling?" We can give the credit to the beautiful peers that have influenced them. In each case, the person who was the positive influence was a church youth group counselor. When we could not agree on an issue, we would remark to our teen, "Go talk it over with Shirley; if she agrees with you, we will change our rule!" "Go talk it over with Ken. We will go with his advice."

Now that we are enjoying our fifth teen, we relax when we see her beautiful college youth leader stop by and invite Gretchen to a Saturday picnic for all the junior-highers. Suzanne is the ideal role model, so it's a great relief when Gretchen asks us for the privacy of a telephone discussion with Suzanne or Steve, the other young college student who gives the positive peer image we desire for our teen. We are not threatened, for we know that these people solve, rather than make, problems. We cannot escape peer pressure, or influence. If the peers are positive, then it's great!

THE GENERATION GAP SYNDROME

For many, the generation gap carries negative overtones of nebulous and confusing parent-teen relationships. Parents dread their youngsters growing up. They fear that our changing world will take their teens so far away that they will become and remain strangers from now on.

May I suggest that the generation gap is what you make it.

Perhaps our teens live in a society that is foreign to us, but does such a generation gap really exist? Basically, life has not changed. The fears, hopes, needs, and desires of teens of the fifties are no different from the teens of the eighties. Therefore we need to keep our focus more on the basic issues and less on the fads that *all* teens experience. Every once in a while, our teens have a "fifties day" at school and they question us about the music that was "in" when we were in high school. We share the ditties still in our memory and we laugh heartily together.

Therefore, our rule is: Deemphasize the generation gap and enjoy it! Yes, the loud rock music is difficult to enjoy when I much prefer my symphony, so we reach a compromise. Since our home is a place of comfort for all of us, we seldom play any music throughout the house, and then only when we all agree upon it. Loud music of any kind (symphony can be very loud too) is a no-no, unless we are home alone or it is confined to a bedroom. Then, we all "give and take" a little to reach a balance. Soft rock is okay if the texts are "positive," and unless our teen becomes so obsessed with it that he or she cannot function without a radio on from sunup to midnight.

Language, of course, causes some intergenerational confusion. More than once, my husband and I have embarrassed one of our children by using a word the meaning of which has completely changed since we were young.

When our son was a teen in the late sixties and early seventies the word for "great" was "boss." Every other sentence was "Wow, that's boss." That same term now has become "neat." "Wow, that's neat!" will be replaced with who knows what.

Become involved in their world, and this parent-teen gulf will be bridged quickly. When Bobby was a junior in high school, he decided to go out for wrestling. Of all sports to choose! We had hoped he would have chosen track or football. However, we decided to take a "positive" approach and become enthusiastic with him in this questionable pursuit. We learned that indeed it was quite a training and disci-

plined art, not at all like the bloody and inhumane displays
we had seen on TV. So we learned the terms and the rules.
When Bobby came home with the scheduling of all his wrestling matches, we had some adjusting to do, for most of them
fell at our revered dinner hour. We wrote them in on my husband's office calendar as "commitments" and the entire family
enthusiastically joined the fan club for Bobby. Little Gretchen
soon learned to yell "Pin him, pin him!" We all cheered for
Bobby to win.

If someone had told us that our entire family would spend
so many evenings of our year missing relaxed dinners at
home, sitting on hard bleachers watching wrestling match
after wrestling match, we would not have believed them. But
we all learned invaluable lessons about being each other's
support system; we learned a new sport, and also enjoyed
family fun!

It's so much fun to be a parent of teens, and there is much
to learn from them. As we share each other's world of fun, I
remember and share with them the joy of my own youth.

Allow me to repeat: We are all changing persons in a
changing world, so we concentrate on the positives and eliminate the negatives.

LEARNING TO FLY

Upon graduation from high school, our children must attend at least one year of college away from home. This was
stressed when our children were only nine or ten, so they
grew up expecting to leave home at the age of eighteen.

It was most important that our children attend a private
liberal arts college that would adhere to the value system we
upheld in our home—a place that would become like a home
away from home, where dormitory rules and standards were
similar to our "house rules." We wanted our children to
"stretch their wings," not just be pushed out into a large,
confusing, uncaring world.

The question we faced then was: How could we afford to send all of our children to college? When our oldest was only five, my husband and I both realized that his clergy salary would never be enough to enable us to send even one child through college. Yet, since both of us had gained so much from our college years, we wanted our children to have this same experience. Therefore, Bob began to write and hoped to publish a book. We would put the money aside for the children's education. His first book, *Move Ahead with Possibility Thinking*, was turned down eleven times before Doubleday agreed to publish it, and it paid for more than one of our children's college education.

Why is this such a strong rule in our home? First of all, we can't measure the importance of this rule in regard to the teenage rebellion that often happens in fifteen- and sixteen-year-olds. Although our teens strained at the parental ropes that kept them from experiencing complete freedom, they knew that in the not too distant future they would have their freedom; therefore, the rebellious feeling was subdued. When our teens would not agree with a rule of being in at a certain time, we often reminded them, "In only another year, you will be away from home, and then you will have the responsibility of *living with the result of making your own decision!*"

"The eagle stirs up her nest, so the young may learn to fly!" is the philosophy behind all the rules and principles of our family. We ask ourselves often, "Will this better prepare our youngsters to live an abundant life in tomorrow's world?" That's what having a family is really all about. The entire training of tomorrow's adults must be the highest priority of today's parents.

How each one of our young people "grew up" when they left home at seventeen or eighteen! So far three have completed their bachelor of arts degrees, but more important, all three have become responsible leaders with a positive approach to doing something to make their world a better place to live in.

When we sent our first child off to college, we did not realize what a difference her absence would make in the rest of the family. The next eldest child became "king" of the family and changed in his personality and in his attitude toward the rest of us. We have now seen four of our children leave, and each time notice the tremendous change that comes over the "now eldest" child at home. We have learned that it is as important to the next child growing up to have the eighteen-year-old strike out on his own, as it is for the young adult to "learn how to fly" for himself.

If there is a final philosophy we try to impress our teens with it is the principle that Bob learned from one of his wise college professors.

"DECIDE WITH YOUR HEAD AND YOUR HEART WILL FOLLOW!"

Our children have heard this principle preached, explained, visualized, and dramatized by their father ever so often.

Above all, we encourage our children to use their heads to rely on common sense in making decisions. "If it feels good . . . do it!" is not the way to discern right from wrong. Serious consequences are averted when common sense wins over impulsive and selfish emotionalism.

Believe in your teens. They are the next generation's hope. You can give them the positive love, joy, peace, and sense of brotherhood they will need to lead their world. Become young again through their dreams, and, above all, enjoy them. Without their capacity for adventure, life would be boring indeed!

9

WHEN THE FAMILY
FACES CRISIS

It was July 8, 1978, a beautiful Saturday. My lovely Korean
hostess requested that her driver return us to the hotel in
Seoul. In an hour's time we would need to be dressed, ready
for a dinner party. On this, our last evening in Korea, digni-
taries were gathering in our honor. Tomorrow my husband
would deliver the last of his lectures. Then we were to fly to
Hawaii, where we would rest in the warm sunshine for a few
days before rejoining our busy California family. We were
looking forward to a short vacation, as the ten busy days of
speaking and traveling through the Orient had tired us. But,
in twenty-four short hours, we would be walking along the
beach, free from the pressures and demands for our time and
talents.

(It is always exciting and stimulating to be guests at international seminars and conferences, but at the same time,
when we come home, we feel completely drained of thought
and inner strength, for we give entirely of time and emotion.)

Already I was beginning to feel the emptiness that comes
with feeling tired, and then when rain began to slow the
traffic and cause confusion, I became anxious to reach the

warmth of our hotel room. Bob would be there, having finished his morning work, and he would probably be polishing up the manuscript for his final assignment tomorrow.

I stopped at the reception desk for the room key, and was told that my husband had picked it up, so joyously I pressed the elevator button, rapidly walked down the hallway to our room and gave the familiar knock. The door flew open and my greeting, "I've had a wonderful day but I am ready for Hawaii's warm sunshine," was not greeted with my husband's usual enthusiastic response. Instead the words had a hollow echo as I noticed my husband's ashen face. He took me in his arms. A member of our staff, who was traveling with us, was taking down information from over the telephone. And in that sudden moment, I heard the words that would change our entire family routine for a long time.

"It's Carol. She has been in an accident. The doctor is trying to reach us," Bob said. I shook my head in disbelief. "She's hurt badly," Bob continued quietly, and more gravely than I'd ever heard him speak.

As he spoke, the phone rang again with a new message . . .

"Carol is in surgery. They are amputating her leg." A shock went through my entire system from the tip of my skull to my toes. Numbly, I walked to the window and looked down through the rain to the people and traffic scurrying over the wet streets. A few moments ago I was one of them, but now the whole world, as I knew it, had toppled upside down.

In years past, as I watched my children leave for school, I often wondered how I might react to a family crisis—death, handicap, cancer, or accident. (Divorce, drugs, and alcohol never entered my mind because there always seemed such stability and security between our four walls. But sickness or accident?)

Now . . . Carol—not our Carol—they are amputating her leg . . . our happy thirteen-year-old, adventuresome, athletic Carol? One of the last chores I completed before we left was washing her softball uniform. Her team was top in the league and she was so proud that she was part of it.

Carol without a leg . . . less then whole . . . what would she—what would we—do? What about the love of her life—her horse, Lady? How could she manage riding horseback, to say nothing of taking care of the corral? Carol? Would she be in pain for long? Was there more that they weren't telling us?

The telephone calls continued and indeed she *was* critical. "Multiple injuries," the message said. What did that mean? I tried to keep my imagination under control. She had been thrown off a cousin's motorcycle on the last night of her visit in Iowa.

The fog began lifting from my mind. Yes, it was only Friday night in Iowa. Tomorrow morning she and Gretchen were to have flown home after a two-week visit to Grandma, uncles, aunts, and cousins. Carol and Gretchen had been looking forward to this trip for months; they seldom had a chance to spend such a long period of time with their cousins *and* on the farm.

Our Carol—so active, so full of life. Can this really be? Without even thinking I began packing suitcases. I needed to get to Carol . . . fast! There were no planes available that night, they said; I still packed. I would be ready whenever and however we could go. If there weren't plane seats available for both Bob and me, maybe one of us could start on the long journey to her bedside, and the other could follow in the morning.

The phone rang again. "The reception begins in ten minutes. There is nothing you can do until we get a plane space for you, therefore it really would be best if you attend."

Again automatically, I ran a comb through my hair, adjusted my dress. Through the next hour I routinely shook hands and attempted to eat. It was an elegant dinner, and we were honored by the presence of many notable people. We were the recipients of much heartfelt love and attention. But my mind was with our Carol.

I kept looking for our staff man. Was there more news? Surely there must be a plane flying out tonight!

Finally, he came with some good news! "We have found

two seats on a Korean Air Lines flight to Los Angeles. We must leave now. Don't worry, I will take care of all the details." He was the first of many angels and miracle workers whom God had "standing by" to help us through this crisis.

The next hours and days remain a blurr of confusion, but beautiful people, many of whom we had never met, guided us around the obstacles that might have otherwise seemed to us like insurmountable mountains. We were given "emergency" treatment all the way. Luggage and customs were not our concern. While the plane was being refueled in Hawaii, we ran to a pay phone to get the latest report. We had no American coins with us, but people were generous. Still, the only message we could receive was "Her condition is stable"! What did that mean? Was she actually fighting for her life? Or was this a routine message following major surgery of any kind? Our questions unanswered, we again ran to catch the plane.

It was dark when we arrived in Los Angeles and another of our staff members greeted us and said, "The doctors say Carol is really fighting and that her attitude is an inspiration!"

I was left with a gnawing stomach. Too much was being left unsaid. We were no longer half a world away. We were in the States and still our staff was giving us no specific information. I again tried to assure myself that everything would work out. And I rested in the knowledge that we were nearly at her side. Again beautiful people were waiting to help us.

"We have a private jet waiting to take you right to Sioux City, Iowa. It is all paid for. I'll tell you all about it later." My thoughts were interrupted by this good news. Again we said a "Thank you, God" for this generous gift, which saved us eight hours in traveling time and airport layovers.

It was four o'clock on Sunday morning when we stepped into the intensive care ward where two of our older daughters were waiting, and then into Carol's room.

I saw her. Our Carol. Her swollen and broken body lay still and white. The stump of her left leg held in traction. Tubes like octopus legs emerged from all parts of her body. She was under oxygen and on a heart monitor.

My heart jumped. How I wanted to hold her in my arms, but I could not. I could not as much as kiss her face. I had to be content with touching her swollen cheek with my index finger. She was injured far more seriously than I had imagined. When we had been too far away to help, they had purposely not told us the worst. She nearly bled to death in the ditch while waiting for the ambulance. But thanks again for the help of beautiful people—doctors and nurses who did not give up when they felt no pulse or registered no blood pressure. They then worked harder than ever. Later, her thick, thick file of medical reports showed that the dedication of these fine medical professionals *saved* Carol's life.

On Monday, Carol's condition worsened and surgery for further amputation was scheduled. My husband and I functioned like robots, hardly able to think clearly, yet making major decisions, but again, beautiful people really made these decisions for us.

We decided to have Carol transported to Orange, California.

On Monday at midnight an ambulance jet set down at the airfield in Sioux City. A few feet away a more conventional ambulance, carrying Carol, approached the airstrip. Quickly, quietly, and expertly Carol was transferred to the plane. Again a team of medical experts showed their expertise; we safely flew to California. There, in the early-morning hours, another ambulance waited for us. We then sped to Children's Hospital, where a team of surgeons from the University of California, Irvine, were ready for surgery.

One hour later, Carol was under anesthesia and my husband and I, exhausted and numb, fell asleep in the waiting room.

Those first days and weeks were filled with excruciating pain and trauma. Surgery and more surgery. High fevers, IVs, and countless blood transfusions. Carol relived the accident again and again in terrifying nightmares. She wanted few visitors besides Bob and me. We took turns staying with Carol. I usually stayed during the nights, and then, during days, being relieved by Bob or another family member, I would go home to sleep for a few hours.

There was no time for me to cook or shop for food. When absolutely necessary, I would throw some dirty laundry into the washer, but our suitcases remained unpacked. Our eleven-year-old, Gretchen, was "adopted" here and there by friends until we saw how badly the lack of her normal home life was hurting her. Naturally, all of our attention had been centered around Children's Hospital, the telephone calls, the mail, "How is Carol?"

But it became increasingly clear that we, as parents of more than one child, needed to be acutely aware of the feelings of the whole family.

All of a sudden, the routine, the stability, the schedule, had been turned topsy-turvy. And for weeks thereafter one of us had been at the hospital. This impossible schedule necessarily began to take its toll upon our normally healthy family communication. Even our married children missed the "normal Schuller routine." At least for me, *everything* seemed upside down and none of us knew what to do about it.

WHEN ONE HURTS, ALL HURT

When one person in a family hurts so badly, all family members are affected. This crisis in our family really helped us understand the difficult challenge of keeping a proper perspective on life—even when things tumble in. Whether the tragedy is death, divorce, disease, or disaster, the focus of the family's life suddenly becomes blurred. It's then easy for parents and children to lose their way.

We found ourselves becoming irritated with each other, although never with Carol. When one of us would forget something, we were easily upset, but we never blamed Carol. We struggled with our changed life-style. I had to turn over most of my office responsibilities to assistants and aides. Helping Carol overcome became the number one goal of the entire family. There was no time or energy left for the many ordinary things that had framed our days with order. More than anything else we missed our daily gathering at dinnertime and the Sunday after-church family get-togethers.

Gretchen grew out of sorts easily and her school grades took a tumble. When she heard that the doctors were scheduling a *sixth* operation for Carol, Gretchen collapsed, sobbing; more surgery meant that I would be spending more time with Carol. There would still be no time left for her. She desperately needed my attention and my hours, but even twenty-four in a day did not give me enough to spread around. The immediacy of Carol's recovery was all-consuming.

During the months of Carol's hospitalization, I told myself, "It will be easier when she comes home. Then everything will return to normal. Our routines will be reestablished." But when Carol came home, a different set of problems occupied my every waking hour.

She was so weak that she was confined to a wheelchair. Having had no experience with wheelchairs, we did not know that some were heavier weight than others. It was some weeks before a visitor clued us in on this information, and thus helped us find a different model. In the meantime, I went to bed each night physically exhausted from lifting the wheelchair in and out of the car, as Carol had to return to the hospital for daily physical therapy.

My day started with preparing and serving Carol's breakfast. When she was able, I helped her into and out of the shower, although during her first few weeks at home, she would crumble to the floor just trying to get to the toilet. The wheelchair would not fit through the bathroom door, and crutches were not yet an alternative. More than once I tried to catch her as she was falling, but then we usually both ended up on the floor, and getting her back into her wheelchair was a feat beyond my imagination. We would cry, then laugh at our situation, as my further attempts to help her often only prolonged or worsened our entanglement.

Later I laid out her clothes, and helped her into the car, then out of the car, into her wheelchair, and into the hospital, where she struggled through her therapy session. How thrilled I was to watch her learn her first important lesson: getting up after having fallen. If she wasn't experiencing too much pain, I would slip across the hall for a needed cup of coffee and short rest. But then we were back to the antics of loading and unloading the car. By the time Carol was settled into her own bed, it was time to fix her lunch. She then rested until the school tutor came.

The job of caring for her was never done. During those first weeks, the ordeal of washing her hair usually ended with a flooded floor, and a soaked mom-and-daughter team. And then, once she was back in bed, who but I was left to mop up the mess? I accomplished little that year besides nursing our Carol back to health.

At Thanksgiving, Carol was back in the hospital, but a four-hour pass allowed her to eat dinner at home. Our usual Thanksgiving crowd of twenty was cut down to include only the immediate family. Instead of attending the Thanksgiving church services, as was our family custom, I concentrated on organizing the festivities to make the most of Carol's visit. I put the turkey in the oven and then each member of the family completed an assignment; setting the table, making the salad, peeling the potatoes, and so forth. I left for the hospital to help Carol dress. She seemed afraid that the nurse might not have time to get her ready for her "release," which was strategically timed to fall between two intravenous medications.

As we loaded Carol into the car, she was nearly beside herself with excitement. She began to cry as we rounded the last bend of the relatively short journey home.

We wheeled her into the house just as the steaming turkey was lifted from the oven (all perfectly scheduled to make the most of her four-hour pass). In a few short minutes we sat around our table thanking God for our unbroken family circle. Our hands tightly clasped each other's; and by the end of our prayer there was hardly a dry eye in the room.

Carol sat at the table only ten minutes before her pain became so unbearable that she asked us to lay her down. She didn't want to go to her bedroom, so, with pillows we propped her up on the living room couch until it was time for her to return to the hospital. She shed many tears that night, because she was so acutely aware of her physical weakness. She could not handle even a quiet family party, yet she yearned so desperately to be home enjoying our company. It would be just a few weeks later—a week before Christmas—when she came home to stay.

And then in January we began the long fittings for her prosthesis and the subsequent therapy to train her how to walk.

Our troubles still weren't over. Getting dressed became a production. When she was wearing slacks, her fake leg would have to be dressed first. There could be no last-minute changes of shoes. Getting a shoe on a prosthesis takes three table knives (not saw edge) in three different areas around the heel. (A shoe horn just doesn't do the job.)

Three years later, there is still adjusting to do. Her bedroom and bath should be reorganized and remodeled to make it easier for her to get around. She still has therapy, and with more amputation this spring she is having her fourth prosthesis made. So far none have adequately fit her, although this problem is not unusual. Obtaining a good-fitting prosthesis is like conquering your mountain: it may take years. It is so difficult because no two amputees are alike.

As Carol has said more than once, "No one can make legs like God does!"

BE PREPARED

When a crisis hits a family, what happens? For us, it meant adjusting our life-style to compensate for Carol's lack of dexterity. We had to learn to deal with new frustrations and their accompanying emotions. Such times include her feeling that because of her leg, she doesn't look pretty when she has a special date, the days when she is late for school because we cannot get her shoe on, or when the heel of her prosthesis breaks. There is the great fatigue that comes from wearing her heavy prosthesis all day. There is the swelling of her stump at times that then hurts so much she cannot wear her leg.

But, thank God, through her childhood, we had emphasized, practiced, talked, and taught positive principles so much that now they are making the difference.

INCH BY INCH, ANYTHING IS A CINCH!

THERE IS NO GAIN WITHOUT PAIN!

WHEN FACED WITH A MOUNTAIN, I

WILL NOT QUIT!

WINNERS NEVER QUIT AND QUITTERS

NEVER WIN!

Brainwashed with positive thinking, Carol's mental attitude holds the key to her determination not to feel handicapped. Since her accident we have again stood on the sidelines and watched her play softball, hobbling to first base after a hit. After the game, she has fallen on her bed, physically ill the rest of the night because of exertion, at times even vomiting, yet she will not give up.

We have watched her try again and again to ride her horse, learning how to mount and dismount. As with her attempts at playing softball, she has overexerted to the point of physical illness, but nothing gets in the way of reaching her goals.

We have watched her learn how to ski on one leg, wanting to fly down the ski slopes in hopes of feeling normal again.

I repeat, positive thinking is not a shallow, Pollyanna, head-in-the-clouds look at life. It is the key to survival when the family faces a crisis. It can make the difference between life and death in illness and accident.

As I mentioned earlier, Carol's will to live kept her alive during the sixty-mile ambulance ride to the hospital. With the doctor's encouragement to "Think life!" and "Fight to live" she pulled through. Her immediate and natural reaction was to *live* and so, with all her might, she fought. There is no doubt in my mind that the emphasis on the positives of life, which we had stressed daily in our home was then paying off.

Our Carol's story is the greatest example I can give of the benefits of a family's immersing their children—from day one —in positive thinking, positive talking, and positive actions.

Last year I was on an assignment for the American Cancer Society and spent a day in one of our nation's cities talking on local television and radio on the subject of Breast Cancer. One of my hosts was an oncologist who served on the local American Cancer Board, and we talked about the stress of cancer on the families of patients. He shared that in the cases he had attended, a very high divorce rate followed the death of a child due to cancer. He went on to explain that the emotional strain plus the physical and financial stress proved devastating, especially if a child had fought a long battle with cancer.

I was deeply saddened by this report and I countered it by telling him about our neighbors who lost their eight-year-old daughter after a four-year fight with cancer. Their marriage and family grew stronger because, in their desperation, they turned to God. Finding a positive faith in a positive God, they found the necessary strength to handle their grief.

As a pastor's wife, I have watched many parents grieve over the death of a child. Those who have had a positive faith in a positive God were the ones who triumphed through a positive attitude toward the tragedy that happened.

I shall never forget the sight of two small coffins, side by side at the altar of our church. On one coffin sat a Raggedy Ann doll. A baseball cap and a teddy bear rested on the other. It was June and one of our wonderful church families of six (counting mom and dad) had eagerly left for a week's vacation. A few days later, while camping, the five-year-old girl fell into a rushing stream. Her seven-year-old brother tried to rescue her. The father tried to save them both, but failed. They returned home as a family of four. What peaceful strength these parents displayed as they spoke only of the goodness of God in having given them the special gift of these children. They triumphed through their adversity.

I have another beautiful friend whose tragedy I shall never forget—a kind, loving, intelligent architect who had lost his daughter years before we met him. She also had drowned. But that was not the great disaster. We watched the father try to drown his grief with alcohol until he died alone one night as a result of his drinking. His death became the greater tragedy in that family.

Words cannot describe the emotions felt when one is completely helpless in the time of crisis. The only way to know these feelings is to experience them. Before the calamity struck, things had always worked out, things had always been "fixable," but now, nothing can make life, as it was yesterday or last year, return. The tragedy has happened—death, accident, divorce, handicap, a son or daughter in prison, financial bankruptcy . . . Whatever it is, it brings with it this total and complete helplessness.

What happens to the family at such a time? Those that look at what they still have and not at what is lost, will again find happiness, peace, and joy. Those families that refuse to feed their mental appetites on negatives will become *better* instead of *bitter* individuals.

When individuals clear their minds of the cancerous diseases of self-pity, anger, and resentment, they begin to heal and learn how to grasp hold of new ways, new ideas. As these positive thoughts take hold in the lives of these hurting people, they become more beautiful on the inside. This radiance then becomes contagious, filling the lives of the remainder of the family, filling the whole home.

Recently an older gentleman was told in my presence that our young teenager was an amputee. He turned to me and said, "Oh, you have a right to be angry!" A little shocked at this reply, I responded, "Why should I be angry? There is lots of living left for our daughter to do and she has some great goals for her future. Carol refuses to give up."

Sometimes when she is in the opposite corner of the house from me, I hear the thump, thump, thump of her crutches. Yes, there were times when each thump flashed a sharp pain through my inner being, but whenever I experience this I force myself to react positively. I turn my mind to Carol lying in an ambulance fighting to live and I can again, in sincere honesty, thank God that she is alive. Now as we hear the thump, thump down the hall, I have learned to laugh about it and even tease Carol: "You'll never be able to sneak in after curfew with such noise!"

The family that maintains a positive attitude during times of crisis becomes a stronger, more beautiful family. They learn that the life of each member is a precious gift, not to be taken for granted. They discover the real treasure of belonging to a family. The family that cries together in sadness is bound together by an unbreakable oneness, for the comfort of a family far exceeds any other security that life brings to us.

IO

NEVER BE NEGATIVE

"No, I am not a speaker. I cannot deliver a speech in front of an audience. I am a musician. I'm sorry, you will have to ask someone else to deliver the report." It was one of the first years of our marriage and my husband overheard my comments on a telephone conversation.

As I hung up the receiver, he was kind but firm as he told me that I could very easily deliver a speech. "You must never say, 'I can't,'" he said. He proceeded to give me ten good reasons why I could write and deliver a dynamite speech. His final encouraging statement was, "Next time say, 'I would like to'; and then I will help you with the details."

When the first speech assignment fell in my lap, it was to a group of wives on the topic "The Positive Approach to Marriage." When I indeed did ask him for his help, it came in the form of one sentence. He said, "Tell them all *Never, never, never be negative.*"

That was the shortest speech I've ever made, *but the most important,* and if there is one single statement that would summarize this book, I would nominate this: *Never, never, never be negative.*" Negative acts, negative words, negative thoughts, are the sum and substance of 99 percent of all difficulty you and I have in relationships with other people. Therefore, with each other in the family and as husband and wife we cannot ever afford to be negative.

POSITIVE NONAPPROVAL

"Never be negative." Does this mean we never disapprove? Of course not: to approve all behavior would be a violation of our basic integrity as persons of conviction and conscience. The positive family will be sensitive to communicate non-approving attitudes positively. We have found that we are positive as long as we respect each other's differences. Preventing a difference from escalating into a real negative scene is simple if we understand at the outset how serious the disagreement is in the mind of another family member. So we have developed a "Scale of nonapproval."

1. The least intense level of nonapproval is, simply stated, "I'm not enthusiastic. But go ahead if you want to." From there the intensity of the comments increases:
2. "I don't see it the way you do, but I may be wrong. So go ahead."
3. "I don't agree. I'm sure you're wrong. But I can live with it. Go ahead."
4. "I don't agree. But I'll be quiet and let you have your way. I can change it my way later on. Next year I can repaint, repaper, reupholster it my way."
5. "I don't agree and I cannot remain silent. I love you but I will not be able to keep from expressing my disapproval. So don't be offended if you hear me expressing a contrary view.
6. "I do not approve, and I make a motion we postpone and delay action until we both are able emotionally and rationally to compromise over positions. Give me more time."

7. "I strongly disapprove. This is a mistake—costly, not easily corrected, and I stand firm. I cannot and will not go along with it."

8. "My answer is no! I will be so seriously upset if you go ahead that I cannot predict what my reaction will be."

9. "No way! If you go ahead I have to tell you 'I quit; I'll walk out.'"

10. "No—no—no. Over my dead body. Try it—and I won't quit—I'll fight back—to the death!"

We respect individual feelings of nonapproval and, if there is a feeling of disagreement, we ask—early, respectfully, honestly—"How strongly do you feel about this, honey?" If the answer is number one, number three, or number ten, we are wiser in how we handle the situation. So disagreements are handled before they get out of hand. It's our way of "being positive" when we really feel "justifiably negative" about an issue or a situation.

THIRTEEN WAYS TO LOVE

How can I know if I'm thinking and being positive or negative? Is there a simple, sure, sensible signal that can tell me if I'm a positive person? Yes! The sign, signal, and source of positive thinking is found in one word: LOVE. Love is a signal that you are "right on!" Love is the source that feeds your positive spirit—and love is the system that really works. There is no better analysis of this key word found in any psychological writings than that found in the Sacred Scriptures in I Corinthians 13.

The most often used and repeated words of love are these: "Love is very patient and kind, never jealous or envious, never boastful or proud, never haughty or selfish or rude. Love does not demand its own way. Love is not irritable or touchy. Love does not hold grudges and will hardly even notice when others do it wrong. Love is never glad about injustice, but rejoices whenever truth wins out.

"Love bears all things . . . believes all things . . . hopes all things . . . endures all things. Love never fails!"

There are what I call thirteen "Never be negatives" in this classic piece of literature.

1. *Love is never jealous.* You and I jealous? Of course not, we know and trust our mate . . . but wait. How often do you go out of your way to give compliments? Did you give one today? *A compliment a day keeps jealousy away.* I've heard husbands tell of jealousy of wives who "get to stay home, plan a leisurely day, and watch TV" and I hear homemakers jealous of their husbands "meeting exciting people at the office and going out to lunch."

None of us are immune to this negative attitude of jealousy. No home is so positive that jealousy does not have to be dealt with in relationships with each other, husbands and wives, parents with children, brothers with sisters, etc.

One weekend, our two eldest children, Sheila and Bob, who were then nine and six, were assigned to wash and dry the dinner dishes, while my husband and I took our coffee to the living room and chatted. The children, upset with this "unfairness," complained all the while they finished their chore. They did not know that we overheard their entire conversation. The negative feelings that poured forth with each washed and dried dish were interesting to hear, especially when they imagined the worst about us. As the one who gave the assignment, my husband received the worst criticism. "I bet when he goes to his office he never works, he just sits around in his office chair!" "Yeah, he has a secretary. You know she types all the letters." Their negative attitude finally reached such astronomical proportions that Bob and I left our easy chairs and joined them in finishing the dishes. We used this opportunity to explain to them what office work really was like. Since they were too young to understand "term papers," my husband suggested that they write a three-page story each day for a week. He explained in great detail that office work was much like going to school every day. What a memorable lesson in negative thinking this was to all of us.

2. *Love is never envious!* How enthusiastic are you about a new idea that is not yours? Our insecurity makes it hard for us to say, "That's a great idea. I couldn't have come up with a better one myself." Too often we torpedo any new idea that is not ours before we even give it a fair hearing.

3. *Love is never boastful,* which means love never exaggerates. Are you in the habit of exaggerating the facts? *"Everything* is going wrong." *"Nobody* is helping me out. There is *no one* I can count on!" *"Everybody* is giving me trouble today!"

Watch out for the *"everybodies"* and *"everythings"* and *"nobodies"* and *"nothings"* in the negative attitude syndrome. They really pull you and your loved ones down in a hurry.

4. *Love is never proud.* Watch out for the negative attitude that arrogantly announces, "I don't need you! I can do it alone!" Yes, we need to be distinctive and independent, but love is never proud and so we think, plan, and act in the positive alternative of the family team: parents are a team, parents and children are a team, each teaming up his or her distinctive responsibility with the others in the success of a happy family.

In our Leadership Seminars, the most difficult mental block to crack is to convince executives that only when they think and work as a team are they able to move ahead in their corporations and businesses. That's why participation in music and sports activities by our young people is so vital to their future careers. It teaches them the necessity of team spirit.

5. *Love is never haughty.* Webster's Dictionary describes haughty as "disdainfully proud; arrogant." I've never thought of myself as a "haughty" person, but then one morning I caught myself using a condescending or put-down tone of voice as I hurried my husband and children out of the house to school and appointments. I've noticed a great deal of "haughtiness" or "condescending" tones as I listen to teachers "teach" pupils, managers "manage" their employees, supervisors "ordering" clerks, husbands talking down to wives, wives talking down to husbands, parents "parenting" children, and

older children haughtily ordering young children. The "I-know-it-all" and "I'm-right" attitude really comes across as condescending, put-down haughtiness. That's a no-no for positive, loving atmospheres because it immediately causes a rebellious reaction that leads to quarrels, fighting, and a "you-can't-tell-me-what-to-do" attitude.

Included in this "never-be-negative" attitude of haughtiness is the sad put-down humor that is so popular today.

Humor in the home is a must. It relaxes and stimulates good feelings and is a soothing healer for any kind of crisis in the home. It's lots of fun to be gathered around our family table when we begin sharing jokes. Early in our marriage we discovered the need to make our days more fun; therefore we encouraged our little ones to share their funny stories at dinnertime. When Sheila, our eldest, was four, she told the same joke every night for months and each time we had a guest we heard the story again—and how she would laugh at her own story. We laughed more at her reaction than at the tale itself.

However, put-down humor, where one is teased and made fun of, is simply cruel. Why is it that we enjoy making fun of someone's big ears, strange clothing, or odd walk? Sometimes we can laugh about each other's eccentricities, but it is a sensitive area that needs much love and caution, so that the result will never be interpreted as a put-down but rather as an acceptance of one another as we really are.

6. *Love is never selfish!* Me selfish? As parents, aren't we always giving, giving, giving? But have you ever said, "I've always done it this way." "I don't want to upset my routine." "My schedule is all fixed and I refuse to change it because I can't handle it!" Who among us is not rigid in certain areas of life? "Don't upset my plans" is a selfish, negative attitude that can become a real block to loving relationships. Are there areas in which you are overly rigid? Can you give in once in a while without becoming unglued?

7. *Love is never rude.* Love is *always* courteous; therefore there is never an excuse for forgetting to say "please" or "thank you" or "may I," but the greatest rudeness of today is

the excuse of being "too busy." I admit my guilt in this area, and I suspect I'm quite typical of most Americans. Everywhere I travel, people are "too busy." Parents "too busy" to answer a child's question. Husbands "too busy" to telephone a wife and tell her "I love you." Wives "too busy" to do a little special something for husbands.

"I'm too busy today; perhaps tomorrow." Love is never rude; are you too busy for love?

8. *Love never demands its own way.* We see it daily in ourselves, our children, our neighbors, friends, and staff: *locked-in thinking.* All of us are experts at building neat little boxes around our theories or rules and are completely close-minded to discussions that might threaten our position. Have you ever heard, "This is the way I was taught; this is the way it will be!" (end of conversation)? Sounds childish and immature, doesn't it? I know a lot of fifty- and even sixty-year-old children who suffer from this negative attitude, and at times I am one of them. Love does not demand its own way!

9. *Love is never irritable!* What kind of vibes do you give? Modern psychology is now intrigued with the aura that surrounds each individual. Have you noticed that you relax with some people while with others you grow increasingly tense and uncomfortable? Are you fun to be with or do you project an irritable spirit?

One morning I overheard the children tell their little friends, "We better play at your house today. Mom is in a crabby mood!" I decided then and there that I did not want to go down in history as a "crabby" person. If it's a bad day, a day when things are going wrong, the final decision to enjoy the day in spite of it all is the decision not to give in to this negative attitude. *Irritability* makes everyone around you miserable. Love makes the children enjoy playing at home. Love makes you fun to be with.

10. *Love is never touchy.* Tension is the root cause of many medical problems. It is a negative attitude none of us can afford to have.

When I gave birth to our fourth child, Carol, my doctor

asked if I was interested in an experiment in "depth relaxation," which he thought would ease the birth process. Having had long and difficult labors with my first three children, I was ready for almost any relief. In the few relaxation sessions I had with him (I was already eight months pregnant), I learned exercises that I still use when I feel tension building up inside my system. Carol's birth was 100 percent free from pain, and so I was convinced I held a fantastic key to health for my inner self.

I first make myself comfortable. Then, with deep breaths, I blow out very slowly all the tension. Next I inhale peace and relaxation. At the same time, with one hand on my opposite shoulder, I pull out the tension very slowly—down my arm, over the elbow, over the wrist, to the tip of each of my fingers. Slowly I draw out the tension, all the while thinking, "Pull out tension, drink in relaxation." Then at the end of the exercise I slowly wipe my forehead and repeat in my mind, "Relax . . . Reee—lax . . . re-laaax." Wow! It works better than an hour-long nap!

Today I often use it in shortened form as I drive in bumper-to-bumper traffic or face a "pressurized" day. *Love is never touchy* . . . relax and stay healthy.

11. *Love never holds grudges!* Ouch! How often do you and I keep count of all the unfair things that happen to us? Sometimes we blame other people, the world as a whole, the "system," or often God. I am often amazed at my own memory and the memory of others. Each detail is vividly recorded in microscopic dimensions. When it is pulled out of storage it is grossly enlarged. We keep detailed score of what he did or she did (or what we thought she did or said), of how we were neglected and thoughtlessly forgotten at an anniversary or birthday. Love does not keep count. "Never let the sun go down on your grudge" is a rule I repeat often. It saves so many heartaches and so much heartbreak. Keep looking ahead and forget the pain of the past. Today is the first day of the rest of your life!

12. *Love hardly notices when others do wrong!* "I'm afraid

to love because I might be hurt again" is another way of stating this negative attitude. Dr. Jampolsky, a psychiatrist friend of ours, teaches that fear, not hate, is the opposite of love. In his book *Love Is Letting Go of Fear,* he states that the most destructive force that chokes out love is the negative attitude of fear. Who does not become fearful at one time or another? Whenever we feel fear coming our way, we know that we need to choose. Will we *love* or *fear?* Each time the choice is set before us, we know that whatever we give out will come back to us. Life is a bouncing ball. Therefore choose to give out love. Love hardly notices when others do it wrong. What can you and I do today that will be a little extra-special love deed to someone in our family?

13. *Love is never glad about injustice.* The last of these thirteen "never-be-negative attitudes" is the antidote to another immature attitude commonly seen in families, at work, and society. How often is it your fault when something goes wrong? Who gets the blame at your house when there is a problem?

"Not I!" "Not I!" "I didn't do it!" "I'm not to blame!"

At the time of a crisis, our defense mechanisms immediately spring into action. We all possess remarkable talent in blaming someone else for what goes wrong.

When we first moved to California, I had great difficulty in adjusting to our new home. I had envisioned a lovely house nestled in orange groves with green lawn and shrubs and orange-blossom bouquets on my table. But when we moved into a home much too small for our needs, it was one of the first in a new large tract. There were no orange trees. No trees at all. There were only bleak gray houses setting on sand— sand everywhere. Even the street was sand. The sun was blistering and there was no cool grass or shade trees. We had no money to buy drapes for privacy from neighbors or carpeting to cover the barren floors.

I thought I was being treated unfairly. Surely I deserved a more comfortable home, and besides, how was I to cope with two toddlers who had no safe play yard? The house was too small, and we had no fenced lawn. The nearby building construction threatened their safety. And how would I keep up with my music without a private practice room? I blamed the builders for not leaving any of the orange groves, the city for not putting in streets early enough, the board members for not giving us an adequate salary, and most of all I blamed my husband for getting me into such an undesirable situation. It was months before I matured enough in my thinking to realize that I was only making matters worse by my negative attitude. I began to change when I started to look at myself in the mirror, saying, "Arvella, the bottom line says that you chose to marry this guy! You knew his work! You were not afraid of adventure and change! So now grow up! Stop blaming everyone else, and accept your situation! Do something else besides making everyone around you miserable."

Beginning with a change in attitude, my energies and time were creatively channeled into finding a solution to my problems. I sought out and found attractive wallpaper within my budget to make our house more homey. I made bed sheets into drapes, I spent Saturdays at auction sales where throw rugs and lawn tools were a steal; I found a local college offering challenging studies in the field of music. But most of all, I made life easier for my husband and children by letting love overcome my negative attitude of injustice.

To sum up my Thirteen Never Be Negatives:

1. Love is never jealous—for if you are, jealousy will make you envious.
2. Love is never envious—for if you are, you'll try to compensate by being boastful.
3. Love is never boastful—or you'll become proud.
4. Love is never proud—or you'll become haughty.
5. Love is never haughty—or you'll become selfish.
6. Love is never selfish—or you'll become rude.
7. Love is never rude—or you'll only demand your own way.
8. Love never demands its own way—or you'll be irritable when you don't get your own way.

9. Love is never irritable!—or you'll be touchy.
10. Love is never touchy—or you'll hold grudges.
11. Love never holds grudges!—or you'll always see how others do wrong.
12. Love hardly notices when others do wrong!
13. Love is never glad about injustice.

Happiness is a choice. Choose to be positive and you choose the success attitude in family, home, career—all of living. Concentrate on the positive emotions and choose to allow them to dominate your life-style.

LOVE—JOY—PEACE—KINDNESS—PATIENCE—GENTLENESS

These are the positive attributes that will transcend all problems and crises.

Choose to have a positive thought, which becomes a positive act, which becomes a positive life-style, and your home will become a place you will enjoy.

11

A HAPPY FAMILY
BEGINS WITH YOU

You can make a decision now to start building a positive family today, even if your dreams have been shattered, or hopes have turned to ashes. Three important action words have helped me immensely to remain positive over thirty years. I've kept them scrawled across the mirror of my mind until they have become etched in my subconscious:

Accept—believe—commit. These healing, hope-generating words drifted across my drugged and drowsy mind as I came out of surgery minus my left breast.

Only three days ago our family was planning a happy, holy holiday to Jerusalem. We were booked to leave in twenty days! We were planning to fulfill a promise we made to Carol one year before when she was struggling to overcome excruciating pain after her accident. Twelve months had passed since those painful days following the amputation of her left leg, when her wounds were deliberately kept open. (This was necessary in order to allow the infection to drain from the debris in her badly damaged thigh.) During the nearly half-year hospital stay, we tried to relieve her pain-filled days and nights by making exciting plans for next summer. "Dad, someday," Carol said, "I want to walk where Jesus walked, even if I only have one leg."

"Carol," her father answered, "a trip to the Holy Land sounds like a beautiful idea. I don't know how well you will be walking by then," he said, "so let's try to make the trip by boat. I'll call immediately to see what's available and how much it will cost."

Within a week, he had made a deposit on the trip, and we talked about and planned the beautiful two weeks our family would be together in the Holy Land.

Now, ten months later, we had our passports and the necessary vaccinations. All reservations were made and paid for. Suddenly my shocking cancer surgery had cast a cloud over our long and carefully planned dream.

"Accept—believe—commit." How many times I had used these three words in counseling other women in their down times? What did they mean *now*? To me? To my family? I had three concerns. Would I be able to look at myself in the mirror and really be able to accept the scar I would see?

What about my husband? Would he be able to accept me this way?

And finally, would I be able to travel in three short weeks?

Would we have to cancel our promise to Carol? For a year the dream of the visit to Jesus' homeland had been a strong encouragement. Must I *accept* the dream turning to ashes? Or must I *believe* that we could go anyway? "*Commit*"—the word was tough, but I knew it was for me. I'd not allow the inconvenience of a breast amputation to upset our family plans! I'd *accept* life with what I had left; *believe* it could be beautiful anyway; and *commit* my hopes and dreams to God.

Five days after my surgery, the oncologist reported that there was no malignancy found in the lymph nodes that had been removed. The liver and bone scans were normal. What relief! They would, of course, continue to keep a close watch on me in the next months and first years.

The tubes were removed, but the heavy bandages stayed

until after I was home for a few days. It was then that a beautiful friend came to visit me. She had had similar surgery some years before and she brought me a most thoughtful treasure. She explained, "In a few days you will go to the doctor to have your bandages removed. Take this gift along. It will help you through your first embarrassment." Inside her package was a breast prosthesis. I did take it with me and after the bandages were removed and the stitches taken out, I dressed as quickly as my arm movement would allow. I determined not to look in the small mirror on the opposite wall until I had put on my blouse, and then I was pleasantly surprised that I looked perfectly normal. As I walked through the waiting room, I caught the admiring glance of the receptionist and I knew I could handle "accepting what I could not change."

The ABC's of happiness were working for me now, too! I was *accepting* myself. We *believed!* We *committed!* Right on schedule, twenty days after surgery, all four of the Schullers, Carol with her prosthesis and I with mine, boarded our ship in Venice, Italy, for a healing and happy inspirational visit to the homeland of Christ.

"Okay, you can make the trip," my doctor said doubtfully. "But promise me, Arvella, that you'll not become too fatigued and that you'll practice your arm therapy each day." Sleeping with an overabundance of pillows and lots of hot showers, I found deep within myself a special strength that surged forward when I took a first step toward *accepting*.

My husband continued to assure me that his love reached beyond my physical beauty. We were so thankful that we had the cancer under control that I began to relax and to even joke about my scars. The girls, in private, would call me their "lopsided mom." When Carol needed to have her leg prosthesis adjusted, I would accompany her to what we called "our spare parts place," where we both had our "spare parts" serviced.

When my loved ones accepted me as I was, I was reminded that I had underestimated their love and understanding.

Accepting, believing, committing: truly a happy family doesn't just happen. It is not the difference of good luck or bad luck. It is not genetically predetermined. It's not the natural result of social status, fame, or fortune. It doesn't naturally follow wealth or health. There is, however, one essential quality that I have observed anywhere I encountered happy families in this world. The quality of happiness is a decision and a determination to be positive, *always* and *any way*.

She had no wealth. Her health left much to be desired. Yet she was rich in happiness because she viewed life, marriage, and her family of six children through positive eyes. She was my husband's eldest sister, Jess.

How we always enjoyed visiting her home. As tenant farmers, they had very little in terms of lovely furniture. Their home did not have running water or other modern conveniences. Their life was hard and Jess suffered from ill health. Although she was not confined to a wheelchair, she spent many days confined to her home. Visiting her was such a joy, for her jolly laughter filled the air as we walked in the door. Sometimes she would apologize because she could serve us only homemade bread with jam. What a treat for us "city folks." But a greater treat was the memory of the laughs we shared together.

ACCEPT

To accept what cannot be changed is the beginning of happiness within ourselves, happiness with those around us, and happiness in a situation we are in that we can do little or nothing about.

Sometimes the easiest exercise that will lead to the acceptance of life as it is today is imagining what life would have been like for us if we had lived in the seventeenth century, the fourteenth century, the first century . . . what would life be like if we had been born and lived today in the Soviet Union? New Guinea? Calcutta, India? Few of us, living in America, have had to survive from day to day searching for food. Few, if any, have been treated like a product, being sold or bartered as slaves.

We can begin our journey to acceptance by making a list of daily blessings that we take for granted. Once a year in our home, everyone makes a list of blessings or assets (one for each letter of the alphabet) for which he or she is thankful. Reviewing this list and adding to it is a mental bath that washes away the negative "I wishes" and "if onlys." The result is a poised and tranquil acceptance of life as it really is.

We have all noticed the immature attitude of toddlers who refuse to accept no for an answer. We have seen teenagers who are unable to accept their long nose or pointed chin. Sheila, our eldest daughter, did not really accept her height as six feet until she married Jim, who is six one. As a teen, when asked the question, "How tall are you?" Her answer would be, "I am five twelve!" She was nicknamed "Jolly Green Giant" by her friends, and they often asked her, "How is the weather up there?"

Every day through every age of life there is a lot of accepting for all of us to do. Accepting is that special ingredient that brings a special poise and beauty to every person, male and female, as middle age brings with it the set lines and the wrinkles where smiles have been.

If we find it difficult to accept ourselves as we really are, we have even more difficulty accepting others (our families) as they are. Wives want to redesign their husbands, husbands want to redesign their wives. Parents want to change children, children want to change parents.

ACCEPT, ACCEPT, ACCEPT. This is the beginning of contentment with ourselves as persons—and the beginning of contentment with our mates and families as they are.

Accepting, then, leads us automatically to the next step of happy living:

BELIEVE!

To achieve happiness with myself as a person, I must believe in my own potential. And only when I am happy with myself will I truly enjoy my family. When I am displeased or embarrassed with my own performance, then I transfer that discontentment onto those I love.

Why do I believe in myself and what keeps me believing in my own potential?

First, I was born into a family where trust and faith were natural elements in the atmosphere. I was nurtured, day in and day out, on these two positive values. As my husband and I have studied the different areas of psychology, we have seen, over and over again, that happiness is not possible without the quality of *belief*. Belief in ourselves, belief in others, belief in the beauty of life, belief in the goodness of our world; all are necessary for life abundant.

What, after all, is the alternative? To not believe is the other option, and to doubt is to become a cynic. A cynic does not dream or set goals. Not believing is having no hope, and when people lose all hope, they die.

How and why do I believe in my own potential? Because I believe in a positive God!

I believe I am a somebody. Made in the image of God, born to make His world a more beautiful place for others. Idealistic? Yes! Pollyanna? That's debatable. But one thing is not debatable: positive belief really works. I know I am having the time of my life watching God's plan for my life unfold. How did I ever get from the farm, as a barefoot girl, to my exciting life in the city? I was not formally trained for the many different functions I now perform, but I move ahead with tremendous confidence, because this positive God is my friend and guide.

There is no place that I can travel that is beyond His care and His love. Therefore, I am confident that nothing can happen to me that, with His help, I cannot handle!

Yes, there has been pain! Yes, there have been tears, but I have a powerful belief in a positive God.

COMMIT

When I first *accept* what cannot be changed, then *believe* that I am capable of doing something great, then I am ready to *commit* my life and set goals for myself!

Last year as I flew back from a speaking trip, I found myself seated next to a seventy-six-year-old gentleman. Striking up a conversation, he began to share not only his age, but his success. With a Ph.D. in law, at the age of seventy-one he enrolled in medical school at Columbia University. He shared how he owned homes in New York, Colorado, California, and Venezuela. When I asked him what he wanted to be remembered for, he responded, "For never quitting!"

Then I asked him about his family, and he shared with me his philosophy on what's wrong with the American family today.

He was emphatic in stressing that "lack of motivation is the major cause of problems in American homes." "Too many well-to-do families fail to motivate children," he said, continuing: "When parents aren't motivated, neither are the children!"

How do parents get motivated? By being accepting, believing, and committed persons themselves. As a high school student at the age of sixteen, I served as an organist for our tiny country church. I had started studying classical organ seriously at the age of twelve, and, since there was a shortage of organists, I began, at an early age, to plan for the Sunday church services.

One evening as I was rehearsing the music for the upcoming Sunday, the words of the song for which I would be ac-

companying the soloist popped off the pages of the hymnal.
Alone, in the darkened church, I played and played the song,
and the words became my prayer of commitment:

> Hold my hand, dear Lord
> Hold my hand.
> I do not ask to see nor understand.
> Only that you will be
> constantly near to me
> Holding my hand, dear Lord
> Holding my hand.

Those words have been my words of commitment for
thirty-six years. They are the reason that I am

> Committed to faith rather than doubt,
> Committed to love rather than fear,
> Committed to hope rather than despair,
> Committed to joy rather than gloom.

Therein I have found an unwavering strength that has
made the difference between happiness and hopelessness in
my life and in our family.

When the *one big commitment* in life is to a higher calling,
then other smaller commitments are easier to make. I knew
that when I made my commitment as a bride, "for better for
worse, for richer or poorer, in sickness and health, till death
do us part," I could, with courage and confidence, know that
my marriage would be blessed by a loving and positive God.

Having committed my life to an all-loving, all-wise, all-
knowing, all-powerful God, I knew I could make plans and
set goals.

"*When you are failing to plan, you are planning to fail,*" is
one of the wisest statements that we repeat in our home. To
write the word "commit" on the mirror of my mind means
that I must plan my life and then work my plan.

I have only one life to live; therefore I must set my mind
and heart on what I want to accomplish. I have always loved

music, and had planned to receive my degrees in music and become a professional musician. But I met the man who is my husband. "Marry me now," he proposed, as he graduated from theological school, "and finish your music studies later." Love won out! Somehow I believed I could have him and my music too.

There has never been a doubt in my mind. I know I made the right choice. Although I still do not have my music degrees, I am using my talent in many areas of music. In addition, I have had the stimulation of attending university classes between babies. Someday, when I retire, I plan to return to my music studies.

I am a happy woman today, for I have *accepted* who I am —and where I have come from.

I am a happy woman, for I *believe* in a big and positive God, therefore I strongly believe that God has a plan for my life. He is unfolding it exactly as He planned—beautifully! And He is helping me to adjust to His bigger plan. (When I look back at my plan as a teen, I was thinking too small.)

Content in God's bigger plan for the one life I have to live, I am able to plan each year, each month, each week, after each day.

On the morning following my mastectomy, before the results of the tests were known, I lined up my husband and the doctor together at the foot of the bed and made them promise that, if the results showed that I had only one year to live, I wanted to know now. I did not want to wait until I was too ill to know I was dying. There were certain things I wanted to do. They nervously shifted from foot to foot, but both men looked at me and said, "We promise!"

A month later when my husband and I were enjoying a moment of reflection and retreat, he quietly asked me, "Honey, do you remember what you made me promise the morning after you had surgery?"

"Aah, yes," was my questioning reply. I wondered why he

could be bringing up the subject. He continued, "I would like to know what you wanted to do if you had only one year to live. Perhaps if it's that important, you should do it."

I didn't know if I really wanted to answer.

It's one thing to know that commitment means having a dream or plan, but to share that dream or plan with someone sets the commitment in concrete! So, I took a big swallow and quietly answered his question.

"If I knew I had only one year to live, I would want to clean all my cupboards and closets, and set my house in order." Since Carol's accident, there has been no time to keep closets and cupboards organized. I didn't think it would be fair of me to leave the family in such disarray. They would have enough trouble adjusting to life without a mom.

The second thing I would do if I only had a year to live would be to write each of the children a special letter, reminding them of special talents and gifts they had that were distinctive.

I would relate to them special events from childhood that they would have forgotten, but that made me very proud to be their mother. Then I would write for them my special philosophy of life. I would write how much I love life, and how much I want to live. How beautiful life can be when we learn to enjoy the beauty around us—family, friends, nature, love, joy. I would write, to each of the children, that the only way to live a happy and eternal life is to believe in a positive God.

Now, two years later, there has been no return of malignancy. Yes, I *have* begun to organize and clean some closets. Just in the past weeks I have been able to reach the top shelves without discomfort, so I now have no excuse. The recovery of complete arm movement has taken longer than I expected. There has been more surgery since that summer so my healing is now complete with a silicone implant and a completely reconstructed breast! I'm not lopsided anymore. My husband tells me (and I know he is sincere), "You are a beautiful medical miracle."

Have I written the letters for the children? Yes and no. I

have written little notes for their birthdays and Christmas. Now that I know I'll live longer than a year, I've stretched out my plan.

I meet many persons of different ages and careers. Those persons who stand out as most unhappy are those who have set no personal goals, no concrete plans for their own personal lives. The happy people are those persons who have it all together. They *know* what they want to accomplish in life. And they know *how* to go after their dream.

I shall never forget one afternoon when a friend whom I admire greatly rang the doorbell. Upon answering I welcomed this member of the church. She came in, quickly sat down, and without delay or emotion firmly stated her purpose for coming and her plans:

"I have just come from the hospital. Don"—her husband—"just died of a heart attack. But I know what I must do. I must go home immediately and sit in his favorite chair. If I can do that, then I know I'll be all right." She allowed me only a moment to express my sympathy. With that, she stood up, smiled a courageous smile, walked alone to her car, and drove away. Today, some twenty years later, she is still a strong, determined woman who is constantly helping others who are going through difficult times. She is still so full of energy and vitality and she has lots of things she still wants to do.

Can you make a list of the goals you want to reach in twenty years? Ten years? Five years? One year? One month? One day?

In a recent seminar for young mothers, I was sharing the goals I had set for this month. I had brought along my "to-do" list for the week. That list has become such an important part of my organized living that I quickly become unglued if I misplace it. I discovered that the majority of these young mothers (mostly in their twenties) had their "to-do" lists also. We had a good time comparing our lists. Though mine differed from theirs, we agreed that the practice of writing down what we wanted to accomplish became an act of commitment, a most important actualization of our positive mental activity.

When we decide *what* our goals for ourselves are, then it is simple to ask *how* we can accomplish them.

Through the years I have continued my goal to have a "be-nice-to-myself" day once a month. How do I keep that commitment to myself? First, I mentally program myself for it. (Half of the fun is looking forward to it.) Then I choose a specific day, writing it on the calendar as a *commitment*. Wow, what this special day does for my self-esteem. Suddenly I find I can cope again with deadlines and interruptions. Sometimes I go window shopping and out to lunch with a special friend. Other times I just stay home, curl up with a good book, and do nothing for anybody from breakfast to dinner. I have gone to an overnight conference where I have no responsibilities, or I go to the beach for the day with my husband, having the mutual understanding that this is a "be-nice-to-myself" day.

Short goals are so important. What may be very unimportant to someone else is of major importance to me, so I make some goals privately with my God.

"She was a good woman." The pastor of the little church in Hawaii exuded love as he spoke about one of the members of his congregation who had just died. He spoke about her good deeds, but I did not hear what he said. I was so impressed with the love in his voice when he said the word *good* that at that moment I made a commitment to be remembered for my goodness. I clearly remember the mental process that took place at that moment.

Would my children think of me as good today?

What did the word *good* really mean?

Do my friends think of me as "a good friend"?

What about the people who meet me as I stand in line at the bank? Or supermarket? The other drivers on the freeway?

"She was a good woman!" Already I had learned of each person's deep psychological need to be part of something bigger than him or herself. Something profoundly deep and significant happens to us when we work totally unselfishly, whether it is in the family, in the church, or in the community.

"She was a good woman!" Will this be said by my family and friends at the end of my earthly life? I daily work toward that goal.

Let me share one more goal. Some reader may find this amusing but I'm very serious about it.

On my seventieth birthday, I intend to run a marathon distance. That's twenty-seven miles! If I survive the run, I shall celebrate my birthday with my family and friends that night. My longest run to date is only seven miles. But without such a big goal, I doubt if I would come near running five miles each morning for the past two mornings as I have, in fact, done!

Are you excited about the family? I am!

Are you excited about life? I am!

Are you excited about being yourself? I am!

The three words that really work for me are *accept, believe, commit*. They will work for you too! ·

Make a list of your goals for this year. Next year. Twenty years from now. And pray along with me this classic prayer:

"Lord, give me the strength to change the things I can change; the courage to accept what I cannot change; and the wisdom to know the difference.   Amen."